Yes I Can!

Louise Cameron Edlund

In Collaboration with Twenty-one Inspiring People Around the World

Publishing History

Edition 1 / March 2020

ISBN: 978-0-244-86855-0

Dedications

I dedicate this book to my loving family, husband, teachers, and tribe across the world. A big *"Thank you!"* to every single person who believed in me in the moments when I didn't know how to believe in myself. Thank you to the ones who fuelled my action from your disbelief in me, as I sprung to action to prove it wrong. I could not be where I am without you. Thank you for my "fierce grace" moment to redirect my life, and to my teachers like Ram Dass, who helped me be able to see the beauty and love all along the way of this beautiful life. Thank you to all my clients who are really always friends in the end. Your support, courage and beauty are deeply touching to my heart and my motivation for service.
~ **Louise Cameron Edlund**

Thank you to my husband, mom, dad, and family for your love and support. Thank you to Abrar and Nadrah for always cheering Mommy. To my amazing clients, thank you for your trusts. To all that read this book, *Yes You Can!* Just do it!
~ **Dr. Izdihar Jamil**

I dedicate this chapter to my wife Heidi, my boys Micah and Asher, my mother-in-law, Elsie, and my mom who taught me to never give up, to live out my passion and do what I love with the people I love most.
~ **Bryan Chamberland**

Dedications

Firstly, I'd like to thank God and my wife for her continuing support and love. She is my Gem! I'd like to thank my family and friends for their continuing love, and I'd like to thank my mentor and editor, Izzy.

~ Chris Tauriello

I dedicate my chapter and all that I create to my beautiful teacher, Liora, who continues to guide me to this day in all that I do. She not only lifted me up from the depths of despair, but she also taught me how to do so for myself and others. She is forever my angel and guiding light. *xoxo*

~ Elle Hari

I dedicate this chapter to the world that is learning my name. Be in competition with yourself, not with me or the person next to you. Be better than who you were yesterday. Remember, your ambition is your main driving force. The highest submit is still to come. Keep climbing.

~ Dr. Hanim Romainoor

I wrote my message for any person that knows in their heart they have a destiny to reach. It's time for you to come out of the "waiting room" of your life and step into the "dressing room" of your purpose.

 No more excuses. Take center stage and shine!

~ Jairrod A. Burch

My chapter is dedicated to anyone who loves to struggle with addiction, to Jason Biggs, Christopher Robbins and Christopher Britton, Emma Faulkner, Brenda Horton, Annie Hillyer, Carolyn Elliot, Sarah Cullham – and you know why!

~ Julie Britton

To my parents, who raise me to beat against all odds.
To my husband, Z, for making this journey possible.
To my children, Hafiy, Fahry, Danny and Irene, without whom this book would have been completed earlier.

~ Lyna Noh

For my husband Paul, who I can be me with, every single day.

~ Maeve Ferguson

To my family who have supported me unconditionally, my partner who has loved yet another version of me, and my one and only daughter, "bean," who has taught me so much. I am forever grateful, darling. X X X

~ Maria Fleet

I dedicate this book to my partner in life, Friderike, and my son Vincent. I love you both so much! To my best friends Volker and Michael who supported me all these years, to my family, to my business partners Patricia and Maud, and the "Diamond Queen" Izdihar for our collaboration, Thank you!

~ Michael Pinto

I dedicate this chapter and book to my dad, mom, and sister. They have always told me to do my best no matter what, and always believed in me, more than I believed in myself.

- Michelle Mehta

Dedications

I dedicate this book to my husband Chris who is my best friend, has held me through every sacrifice, kept laughter in my heart, been the most wonderful father and chosen to experience all that this life has to offer alongside me. He is my soulmate and friend thru all eternities.
~ Nuala Taylor

I truly want you to experience Healthy Living, Inside and Out with a healthy mind, a healthy body, healthy skin and a healthy business.
~ Pix Jonasson

I dedicate this book to the three most important people in my life: my beloved sister Leslie, my amazing husband Taylor, and our greatest joy and love – our little boy Elvis. Thanks to my parents for raising my sisters and me with the ethics of hard work and love of family.
~ Rina Pineda Strauss

For the one who refuses to accept things as they are.
~ Ronica Brown

"Give thanks to the Lord for he is good, His love endures forever" (The Holy Bible, 1 Chronicles 16:34). In everything, I do, my biggest support after the Lord is my husband . Thank you, Raj, for all your unconditional support.
~ Snehal Singh

I dedicate this book to my clients. I promise to help you stay motivated and inspired during our time together. My quiet powers as an introvert with a shot of extrovert, allows me to come from a place of curiosity, gratitude, authenticity, and straightforwardness in my approach. I will help you identify networking and event opportunities to help you elevate your experience.

~ Tequila Cousar

I am thankful for my mother; she is a huge part of my success. She is always there for me and very supportive. She believed in me even when I didn't believe in myself. I am thankful for my four sons. They taught me how to love and to be a better parent. I am thankful for my family, friends, clients, and future clients.

~ Tracie Osborne

I love findings the truth of something. Research drives me into that. Now that I have practiced some of the effective techniques in preparing successful grant proposals, I would like to share with other researchers throughout the world.

~ Dr. Wahidah Hashim

Book Reviews

"Such a nice story of failure and eventual success from Izdihar that really resonates. The super-simple Client Attraction Accelerator method she came up with is genius!"
Miha Matlievski – The Fail Coach, Europe

"I recently met the amazing Izdihar via another consultant/coach friend of mine and she kindly offered me to read this story.

She's 100% right, it's the power of not taking a No personally and realising that 3% of people are ready to buy from you today... maybe it's actually 1%. The fact is, when you make a committed decision to achieve something, you'll have many tests, many doubts, many moments where it seems impossible... I personally know this well, but if you follow her advice, you'll discover you can have anything your heart truly desires.

Our mind can either run our life or we can run our mind and control our life... you choose!"
Brett D. Scott – Success Coach, Australia

"Izdihar is an extraordinary money coach. She walks the talk. A powerhouse and a massive result producer. Indeed, rejection can be a blessing. I highly recommend her as your business and money coach. She will create magic and miracles with you!"
Dr. Sawiah Jusoh, Entrepreneur, UK

"What I love about this book is that it is not pushing one particular viewpoint, it is a collection of real stories of people who have conquered difficulties and setbacks to achieve success. Inspiring and authentic."

Gill Warren, Entrepreneur, UK

"What an amazing read!!!! Heartfelt, honest and authentic, I could feel the rollercoaster of Dr Izdihar's emotions. She captures the essence of our deepest fears and shows us how to overcome them with practical, actionable steps. A must have for everyone but especially aspiring entrepreneurs."

Dr. Amber Qureshi – Dr. Amber Q: The Health and Mind Specialist, London, UK

"Yes I Can! is a complete mind shift and the new normal when it comes to embracing rejection. My biggest takeaway: "Anything is possible, right?" *I agree 100%."*

Cordelia Ghaffar – Health & Wellness Coach, USA

"This is one of the best books to read for all entrepreneurs. This book opened so much of thinking ways in my mind. No matter at what stage you are, you have to read this book at least once. For all beginners to established owners, this is must book in your personal library. I understood so many things, which I may get at 40's, by just reading this. Cheers to author Dr Izdihar Jamil. Thank you for sharing all your learning."

Nakul Chandra – Digital Strategist & Business Consultant, India

"I finished reading with the feeling that I had learned a lot effortlessly. Dr. Izdihar Jamil and her expressive style of writing is very eye-opening, inspiring, and enjoyable to read."

Zurlia Servellon – Business Coach and Author of the Bestseller *the Hidden Patterns of a Successful Mind*, USA.

"Very encouraging and empowering book. It's very true that rejection is part of the process and it's a way to correct ourselves. It teaches you not to give up on your dreams and to keep going after what you want no matter what others might say or do. Great book Izdihar!"

Samah Alzyoud – Business owner, Canada

"In her new book, Izdihar Jamil shares the humble and unlikely story of how she moved across the world to pursue her dreams. She shares her ups and downs on the journey to becoming the online sales queen that she is today. With her presence she is showing up to teach and guide her tribe to greater prosperity. Her energy and vibe are a powerful inspiration to anyone who is doing high-ticket selling."

Gunhild Schou-Bojesen – Business Mentor and Course Creator, Denmark.

"Wow! This was such an inspiring book with game changing concepts to open up the mindset for anyone about to embark or currently on their entrepreneurial journey. A must read for those looking to skyrocket the progress this year."

Catherine Fitch – CEO, Global Evolved Brands, Ltd, United Kingdom

"The inspirational stories in this book made it an easy read."

May Naik – Director of Naik Antiques and Oriental Gifts, Malaysia

"Izdihar is such an inspiration as an entrepreneur and coach. Her personal triumphs help remind us that, with enough perseverance and the right business systems, each of us has the ability to create the abundant life we've always dreamt about!"

Jessie Sawyers – Author of *Getting Unlocked: How to Evolve Yourself Through the Power of Self-Love*, USA

"Wow! Izdihar explains how to reframe the devastation of rejection into the fuel that powers your progress. She lays out a step by step process to help you turn your rejection into correction to your destined success!"

Tommy "Mr. Enthusiasm" Lanham – Personal Alignment Specialist; United States of America

"If you're someone whose constantly second guessing yourself, and your own limiting beliefs and lack of self-confidence are stopping you from hitting your goals, then you have to read this"

Lloyd Yip – LWY Consulting, Canada

"Achieving success is never a straight path and Izdihar's story is a testament to that statement! Izdihar shares her fascinating story of grit, resilience and persistence that enabled her to be the successful business coach that she is today! And to top it off, she accomplished this whilst being an amazing mom and wife!"

Akhil Viz – Business Owner, USA

"A must read for anyone starting or running a business. The book features stories of incredible courage despite the odds, a reminder if you want to succeed to never ever give up. Truly inspirational."

Ivana Katz – Owner of *Websites 4 Small Business*, Australia

"I had the opportunity thread the first few pages of Dr Izdihar Jamil's upcoming book. I found myself smiling all the way through. here we have this woman, new to the USA and jumping in with both feet with her very own business. And that 'both feet" thing is critical…She knows what rejection is but keeps moving forward…It's a beautiful thing."

Jim Brown, Entrepreneur, USA

"Such a great read and reminder to keep going and decide that you'll succeed!"

Rikke Hundal – Entrepreneur, Denmark

"Some things are just foundation… Read this, make a note, post it on your mirror and review every day! If you were looking for a sign - this is it. If you wanted the secret sauce - you found it!"

Kat Halushka – Profitable Speaker Bootcamp, Canada

"Bryan's message is honest, powerful, and practical. If you work the success actions, the actions will work for you. A must-read for anyone who wants to create a prosperous and purpose-driven life!"

Oscar C. Guerrero – Founder & CEO of Social Proof Media, Inc. and Confidence Coach

Book Reviews

"Bryan is one of the most passionate people I have ever met. You can't help but smile and be inspired as you spend time with him, listen to him and learn from him."

Jonny Holliday – The Robb Nash Project, Musician/Artistic Director, Canada

"We all face different kinds of adversity in our lives. Optimism is the most powerful tool we have to get through it. Bryan has experienced extreme adversity, and his endless supply of optimism has taken him out of the depths and on to new heights. Having worked with him for several years, I've seen it in action. The information and techniques he shares here are priceless and life-changing."

Brian Moylan – Three-time Emmy-Nominated Media Designer, Canada

Table of Contents

Introduction

When you look at successful people, have you ever wondered what their secrets are that made them so inspiring? So inspiring, that no matter what happens, they keep moving forward? They seem to just keep expanding their comfort zone and getting more successful. Wouldn't you love to know their secrets so that you can be empowered in your lives too?

The secrets and strategies presented in this book aren't just fancy theories. They have been tested out by real people – just like you and me. More importantly, they produced significant results and have helped them to be successful in their respected fields.

Life isn't just about unicorns and roses. We have challenges, dramas, and opportunities. The biggest difference between successful people and ordinary people are the actions that they choose to take despite circumstances.

Success leaves clues. In this book, we will be hashing out the success secrets from 22 inspiring people around the world. The people in this book have walked the path of your story and not only survived but thrived. Some may have been in a much worse condition than you, but they were unstoppable in shifting their life around.

This book brings you the stories of 22 inspiring people from various backgrounds, cultures, and upbringings and will shine a light on what's possible in your life. Success leaves clues. When you implement the ideas and secrets in this book, they will lead you to opportunities and a brighter future.

So, have faith and believe with all your heart that
    "*Yes I Can* Do This!" and success will follow.

Love,

Izdihar Jamil

Yes I Can!

"Rejection is a blessing. It's just a correction towards your destined success."

Louise Cameron Edlund

Trust the Journey

Louise Cameron Edlund
Soul Development Coach, Ibiza

"Nobody knows what you need to do for your
life better than you. You are the master of
your life. The power really is within you."

~ Louise Cameron Edlund

What if I told you that I, the woman behind the miracle
business of unlocking peoples' full potential and guiding
them to do, be, give, have, and become more than they ever
thought possible, was once very lost and confused in life?
Would you believe me? Would you begin to feel the truth so
deep within your being that within you is the power to create
anything you desire for yourself, those you love, and the
world?

The Unthinkable

*"How do you do it? How do you see right through me with
your laser perception and speak words that seem to go so
deep to my soul? You have such a soft, peaceful, and yet
so powerful presence to you. Is this simply the outcome of
some seriously good training and experience, or do I sense
there is something more to your story?"*

This is the conversation one of my coaching clients curiously explored with me one beautiful sunny autumn day at my home in the Mediterranean paradise island of Ibiza.

Picture the scene. The sun was shining the golden morning light onto my face, and my skin was radiant, clear, and makeup-free, allowing my health and vitality to shine from the inside out. The wind was gently blowing my glistering blond hair and my floating Ibiza goddess-style dress. I was literally in my element and living my most-fulfilled life.

I smiled at her as I sipped on my cliché herbal tea, but with a mischievous sparkle in my blue eyes.

Meeting my mischievous glance with her smiling eyes, she continued her playfully inquiry, *"The million-dollar question that I want to know is, are you literally an angel sent from the heavens or do you have some kind of magical secret?"*

Her question made me laugh, and I replied with a smile, *"Perhaps a little bit of both."*

You see, there is a secret. There is a secret to the woman I used to be, and a secret process that got me to the woman I am today. The biggest secret of all is that there are no secrets. In this chapter, I will reveal all.

What I learned on my journey changed my life, and it can change yours too.

So, this is the part where I utterly shock you and let you in on some juicy details of my life. While writing this, I can't help noticing how easy it can be for us to automatically look for the worst in ourselves to share first. The mind can do that, you know, look for the negative first. Some scientists even have a theory that it is a program running in our brain, designed to look for the dangers (negatives), like the big snake or spider in the jungle days.

This might also be down to the fact that I was born and raised in beautiful Scotland. The land is "bonnie," and the people are famously friendly and modest.

For the above reasons, I am beginning my personal practice of learning to look for the positives first and practicing not being so shy and modest to share those parts of me. So, before I go for the shock factor, I would like to share with you a couple of strengths that the previous version of myself had.

- I was good fun. Having undiagnosed dyslexia as a child, and not having individual learning support at school, made getting through my schoolwork a little bit of a challenge. I discovered that instead of struggling on with my schoolwork, it was much more fun to talk to connect with the other children and laugh. Having fun was something I carried with me throughout my life.
- I also had a vision that life didn't have to be ordinary and the same as what everyone else wanted to do. Life could be extraordinary, and your very own creation of it.
- I always had a very empathic soul and was always ready to be there for you.
- I was intelligent and caring, studying my BSc degree (with honours) in physical therapy with a desire to learn to help others.
- I was daring and strong, setting up my own business the first year I left university at the age of 21.

Ah, there you go. I did it. The sharing of the positives about myself used to be a very uncomfortable practice. As the saying goes, "feel the fear and do it anyway." There is a lot of room for growth in the space of discomfort. Train your mind to look for the positives in life, yourself and in any situation. Trust me; they are always there, even if the spider does crawl by.

Now to the more shocking part of this story. How I, the angelic being from my client's vision, began her journey might not exactly be what you had in mind. Can you imagine finding me in five-inch, killer heels, a short, skin-tight Hervé Léger bandage dress, false eyelashes, a face full of makeup, a glass of Champagne in hand, and a table full of NBA players? Would you believe it was the same person?

The Conflict

It's not that there's anything wrong with the image I once had; it's just that it was never really me. The problem back then was that I had no idea as to who the "real me" really was, and so I played a role.

Now, we all play a role in this world. The question to ask is, are you consciously creating who you are being with decisions, visions, and actions coming from a centered and connected place that reflects and channels the innermost part of you, the essence of your soul? Or, are you unconsciously investing into other people's ideas and visions from movies or advertisement models, and unconsciously making choices to channel an external image of someone that does not actually reflect the "real you," the unique and wonderful being within?

At this time of my life (in a time before the world of *Instagram* influencers), I was unconsciously projecting an image I was borrowing from the outside world, something that belonged more to a Hollywood movie or rap video than my innermost truth, the essence of my soul.

Below are some other side effects to not living a life truly aligned to my individual truth. Perhaps you can relate to one, two, three, or all of the below. If so, congratulations. It seems you are also alive, and very much a human being figuring yourself out on this journey of life.

- Ticking all of society's boxes, without feeling fulfilled in life;
- Confusion of who I was, where I was meant to be, and what I was meant to be doing in my life;
- Experiencing suffering from not knowing how to understand my feelings and emotions, and numbing the suffering with distractions, partying, shopping, overworking and so on;
- Having a lot of outside false confidence, to mask my inner, low self-esteem;
- Low self-esteem was reflected in relationships by being codependent on gaining love and validation from others, yet not even knowing how to let love in;
- A desperate need to create changes in the outside world to make me feel better or more fulfilled on the inside. Happiness was in the next place, person or shopping trip;
- Feeling like I needed someone or something to fix me, always giving my power away;
- Feeling that life was sweeping me through its fast-flowing river, with no raft and no paddle;
- The feeling inside that life could be different and extraordinary, yet not knowing how to break free from my own limits and fears;
- My mind felt like a washing machine going through an endless spinning cycle;

- My low self-worth and feeling of being out of control of my life manifested in an eating disorder.

I invite you to take a full expansive big breath in and releasing breath out if you relate to any of these points. As I said, this version of me was still pretty amazing (as are you). Let's not forget her determination and the vision that we have the right to experience the joy of living an utterly extraordinary and fulfilled life.

The Breakthrough

This is normally the point of the story where people share their breakthrough moment. One day you suddenly connect to your heart, wisdom, highest vision, and get yourself on track, right? This has for sure happened to people and is also entirely possible, in fact, it's how I work with my clients, but it seemed that the universe had some work for me to do. My enlightening breakthrough moment did not happen this way for me.

My breakthrough message wouldn't be heard until I was still and silent enough to hear it. I was the type of person saying, *"Show me the signs."* Signs would come at me from all angles, hit me on the head, and I still was not present enough to see them. And so, for the anxious, city social butterfly that I was, it took the great force of a car accident to stop me in my tracks.

This seemingly dark and terrifying event in one's life is what my great teacher, Ram Dass, referred to as "fierce grace." I desperately yearned for change, and yet I was so terrified of it at the same time, so this fierce grace swept through my life, not to scare me, but to redirect my life back on its true track. It did take me a little time to see things that way, that's for sure.

I had chronic pain in my neck and upper back, hypermobility in my lower back, and wasting muscles in my right leg. This forced me to give up running and all the high-intensity workouts I had done to keep me sane, to blow off some steam. Doctors, fellow physical therapists, and MRI scans were uncertain of what the future would hold for my body and if it would return to normal function.

What did this mean for my life? I was plunged into the dark abyss of uncertainty and fear. There was no edge to hang on to, no place to hide, nothing I could distract myself with – it was time. It was time to be still and face what I had unknowingly been running from for most of my life. There was a person I was forced to face in these conditions, and this was the most terrifying person to me. This person was myself.

Now I could tell you a lot about the physiology and mechanics of the body as a physical therapist. With all my knowledge and experience with the body, I could find no tool in my toolbox to help me with all of the emotions and processing I needed to do.

In a moment of absolute utter desperation, I turned to the last thing in the world that I ever thought I would do. I went to my first yoga and meditation class.

The results were so utterly profound and transforming for not only my body and my mind, but for my emotions and my soul – a word I had never uttered – but I had finally found her.

This journey had sparked such curiosity in me that I began to read books on Buddhism, mindfulness, and personal development. I came across life-changing teachers that would provide the road map and directions out of this dark space and into the light.

Finally, I had connected and found home within myself.

As the rawness of the event settled, and I discovered this connection to myself, there is only gratitude for the unmistakable gift that was to be found in my fierce grace moment. Without this happening, I would not be the woman I am today.

The more I explored the ancient eastern practices, the more I unraveled the truth that human beings are multidimensional, to fully heal any person we must approach this with a holistic plan. In the ancient texts to heal is to become whole within your being. It also became clearer to me that we are all extremely unique and wonderful individuals. It seems we all have a unique message and gift to bring to this world. To connect to your soul is to connect to your purpose for being here in this beautiful life. If you are alive and breathing on this Earth, you are so profoundly important and needed here. You really have the power to create profound positive change in yourself, those you love and the world.

"And all this from yoga and meditation?" you might ask? Pretty much. It certainty began the journey where the inner mystic meets the scientist; it was the catalyst for deep transformation. It was the beginning of discovering the resources to change my world, from the inside out.

But I was a scientist, a physical therapist. Just an ordinary girl with an extraordinary world opening up within her.

Was there a way to share this with my peers and not be looked at strangely? Where could I possibly go with my life from here?

Let's just say the signs kept on coming, and I kept on missing them. Along came my second saving grace moment. A lorry drove into the back of my car, my second car accident.

I decided to take some time out and go to Costa Rica. There, I had a major life epiphany while in a cactus labyrinth with my yoga teacher and a man playing a didgeridoo to the setting sun (as you do). I was going to become a yoga teacher and explore how I could bridge the gap between the physical body, mental body, emotional body, and spiritual body. I had to share this and support people coming into their wholeness. I knew the benefits I could bring to the world, and I was ready to share.

Crossing the Threshold

I picked a beautiful little paradise island in the Mediterranean Sea. Although famous for its nightlife, and, of course, I had definitely been there for that side, it is also famous for its majestic energy and beauty.

The perfect spot.

Let's just say the majestic energy of the island did not disappoint. During the training, I had a lot of space to connect to myself. Add onto this the alchemy of the yoga practices and the breathtaking surroundings of Ibiza. The very loud voice of my mind began to find a new stillness and a new softer voice began to emerge from the core of my being. I recognised this voice, like a very old, trusted friend.

I had witnessed her speak a few times in my life. She would tell me to call a certain friend who had just been thinking about me and really needed to connect. She would guide me to turn left out the shop when I had planned to go right, and I would happen to bump into just the right person. Come to think about it, I think it was the same inner guidance that led me to Costa Rica and to book on this training. For me, this voice was not spoken in words, but in feelings. I guess this is what they call my intuition.

It turns out the connection to my intuition would ask me to change the entire course of my life – to stay on this beautiful island, to leave my city apartment, to leave my business, to leave my loving family, to leave everything I had known, and to leap into the complete unknown.

And, so I did.

I left that teacher training a free woman, with nothing but a suitcase and a dream. And oh, boy, did the dream unfold!

What happened from this point onwards could be a book of its own, so let me give you the short version.

Meeting the Mentors

A beautiful, handsome, Swedish man came into my life. He was not just any regular prince charming, the one who would ride over on his beautiful stallion and sweep you off to safety (although there were times of that). He would get off the horse, hand me the reigns, and tell me I was strong enough to get up there myself, to ride away on my own magical adventures. And the times I wasn't strong enough to do it on my own, he would be by my side and supporting me until I found the strength. I really thought I would fall deeply in love with him and find eternal love in him, but what happened completely surprised me – he helped me to fall in love with myself. Falling in love with myself meant I did not need to rely on anyone filling up my love cup. It was an overflowing cup of love within me, available at any time.

Of course, I married such an angel. Together, we began the love story of falling deeply in love with ourselves. The more capacity we could find to love ourselves, the more capacity we had to love the other, without conditions. There was a "newfound spaciousness in togetherness," as Khalil Gibran would say. Learning to fall in love with myself changed not only my relationships but also my business. When you love yourself, you value yourself; and when you value yourself, you invest in yourself; and when you invest in yourself, the value you can bring to people's life increases and the more value you bring to people's life, the more value they place in your work.

My prince charming and I had countless adventures together. I was beginning to value myself for sure, but there were still a lot of unanswered questions that I had. You know, the big ones? Who am I? What's my purpose? What's the purpose of life? How can I make life fulfilled and extraordinary for myself and those I love?

And so, we went to the sacred mountains of the Himalayas and the motherland of yoga – India. For four years, we lived half of the year there during the winter and spring season. I immersed myself in the teachings of the masters. To describe the diverse and complex teachings of ancient science, mysticism, and philosophy, in short, they were all directing me inward. They always directed me to come back to the present moment. It's actually all that exists, so if you want to change your future or to overcome your past, you must invest in your present moment. You must be creating what you want in the future in the now, the only place that both exists and is guaranteed. Clean the vessel of your body. Clean the vessel of your mind and receive all the wisdom and information that you seek to find on the inside.

The masters sure did seem to know what they were talking about, but just to be sure, we also visited the tribes of the Amazon Rainforest. They were also directing us to stillness, to nature, to our own power within, *"You are the medicine" "You can heal your life."*

We even travelled to Hawaii to learn from world-renowned Buddhist and spiritual teachers such as Jack Kornfield and Ram Dass. It seemed they all agreed. They were teaching the art of going inward – of practicing deep, loving acceptance of who you are; to become friends with your thoughts, your mind, and your emotions; to understand, to transform, to transcend, and to grow. Each and every single person is worthy and capable of living life with deep peace and fulfillment, and there is nothing to prove to be worthy of that. Your existence is enough; it's there for you to feel at any time. Lean back, lean inside and connect.

All the teachings were directing me to who I had been looking for, and at the same time, who I was running from – myself.

The power to be, do, have, give, and become whatever we want is in our very capable and powerful hands. We are conscious creators of our life. We are the artists, the world is our canvas, and our life is the masterpiece.

So, if we all have the power to shift and transform our feelings and emotions, to always have the choice to be in peace, and if we all have the power within us to create the life we desire and be who we truly are within if we really do have a message and it really does matter, then why is everyone not expressing their true colours out to the world? Why, when I look around, do I see so many people not fulfilling their soul's desires? If only they could see what I see, how different would the world look?

Soul Growth

It became clear to me that the biggest injustice in this world is that we are all given this incredibly magical gift to experience and express life, and we only get one of them (or at least in this lifetime as the mystics might add) and yet not everyone is aware of what a gift life is, what a gift they are to life.

My mission would be to learn whatever I needed to learn, from the training of my mentors to the inner wisdom I hold within my cells. I must support people to realise their truth and live a completely fulfilled and extraordinary life. We can change the world from the inside out.

I studied ancient breathwork strategies, releasing trauma from the field of our body, meditation, life coaching, neuroscience, body and mind connection, just to name a few.

The Reward

Having gone on my journey from my old anxious and confused life to crossing the threshold and leaving all that I knew for a profound and truly transformational miracle shift, meeting my mentors, overcoming the old patterns, I found myself on the other side with the reward – my new "superpowers":
- Intuition
- Laser perception
- Clarity of thought

- Presence
- Wisdom
- Serenity
- New Perspectives
- Spiritual guidance
- Multidimensional holistic approach to my work
- A return of a fully functioning body
- Aligning body, mind, heart (emotions) and soul (purpose/ talents)

Perhaps the biggest superpower discovered was simple gratitude for being alive. Can we all take a moment to just remember that life is one of the most extraordinary things in the entire universe? If you are alive, you have the biggest superpower of all, life. You breathe in oxygen that is provided to you by the trees. You breathe out carbon dioxide and the trees take that in. In just one breath, you are part of an incredible miracle.

There is nothing that makes me special. We are all equally extraordinary in our own ways. Each and every single one of us brings a unique gift or talent to this world, and each one equally needed. Did you know that there are around 9 different ways of expressing intelligence? Perhaps you went to a school that only knew of one or two ways to express intelligence, and perhaps your superpower was overlooked? As Albert Einstein wrote, "Everybody is a genius. But if you judge a fish by its ability to climb a tree, it will live its whole life believing that it is stupid." If you are aware of your unique gifts, thank you for recognising them. If you are not aware of your unique gifts, I invite you to reflect on what the gift that was overlooked might have been - get curious.

Life is an incredible journey. I was given an opportunity to learn what I know not only from reading and learning concepts. I also had an opportunity to experience putting the wisdom into practice , to learn from experience and witness firsthand the results. I have walked the same very path that those I support will walk. This has allowed deep and intuitive connections to form between those I work with. This is the ultimate reward.

Through working together with my "superpowers," my clients are transforming their reality to activate their "superpowers" and make a positive impact on the world. By working together, they have made deep shifts that have enabled them to see their own world differently. When you see things differently, you gain new perspectives and clarity of mind and things change. You show up differently in the world, and you begin to create what you had previously thought was impossible. It's entering into a new experience of your life where the limitations are only in your mind. Your world becomes limitless with boundless opportunities.

Just like for me and my life, the impossible becomes possible.

My clients have more time to spend with family and loved ones as they value their time more. My clients learn the true value of who they are and how they can serve in this world. Personal development increases your capacity to grow. The more you develop, the bigger your impact in your service. The more impact you make, the more valuable it becomes. This leads to fewer hours working, life fulfilment, more money earned, and a greater positive impact on the world.

Can you imagine a world in which the millionaires were conscious human beings determined to support and grow a positive future for all?

Your extraordinary life of fulfilment is yours to create. It's a creation of your visions. It's your very own millionaire lifestyle of perhaps infinite love, infinite health, infinite community connections.

The more you serve yourself, the more you serve your world. Keep believing in your visions and yourself. **The Deepest Truth**

I am here to tell you that it is possible. Your visions, your dreams, your goals, and living a truly peaceful, abundant fulfilled, and extraordinary life – it is all possible.

You really can have it all.

Are you ready to reclaim your power as the conscious creator of what you truly want for this world, this one precious life?

You might be expecting a list with THE secret formula. I would love to give you that, and if you choose to read on, I will share, but before we move on to that, there is one thing – that list does not fully exist. There is no one right formula because we are all unique and wonderful beings who have our own unique path, with no real right or wrong way to do things. There is a Chinese proverb that explains, *"There are many paths to the top of the mountain, but the view from up there is always the same."* My job here is not to tell you what to do, or even to suggest how I did things is how you should do things. No one knows what's better for you and your life better than you do when connected to your core. I see you and I see that vision you hold within your heart. I am here to tell you that the world needs you, more than ever, to believe in yourself and your visions.

And that's what I am really here for, to help you connect to your own wisdom-keeper, guru, and master within. I am here to support you on walking your own path, providing you with some navigation tools.

You were born here to be the master of your own life. The process of working with me is to reawaken that truth within you in a fully safe, held, and supportive space.

Now, take 10 long, full, and expansive breaths in, alternating with 10 fully releasing and relaxing breaths out. Now let your breath come back to its natural flow.

You are so worthy of creating all that you desire for your world, but may you also rest in the truth that you are perfect in this very moment. There is nothing to prove; you are already enough. If you ever feel overwhelmed, like there is too much to do, be done, transformed, or changed, may you rest in the peace that everything is perfect as it is.

Knowing this is a very important ingredient in the recipe of the paradoxical nature of life. True soul-level success is a dance between the doing and the being, the actions and no actions, the giving and the receiving, the energy that drives us outward and forwards to create the change we desire, and the energy that draws us inward to our centre where everything is perfect as it is. Carl Jung refers to the peace that comes from taking the middle road.

Wisdom, Insights and Inner Master Navigation

Now that you are aware that there is an alchemic dance to be made for creating a true abundant reality, that your purpose is both to simply be alive and also to fulfil your unique soul-level desires if you choose. Now that you know that you are the master of your life, and all the power is within you, you are ready for the next step.

The next step is on your unique path – I will share my self-navigation system to direct you from where you are to where you wish to be.

Here are some of my reflections and self-navigation questions to strengthen your wisdom and insights for achieving your onward journey. Whilst I mentioned there is no right or wrong, you might think of life as a game - or as the Sanskrit texts suggest the "*Laila*" (play of the gods). And every good game does have some form of guidelines. Feel free to explore these shares as simply some guidelines to help you maneuver in your game of life. If something feels right, use it. If something does not, place it to the side and explore your truth.

Reflections

- Love yourself. Everything good will come from this place. The more you love yourself, the more you look after your body and mind. The more you look after your body and mind, the more self-worth you have. The more confidence you have, the more productivity you will experience. All this will be reflected in your improved relationships, finances, and life freedom.

- The moment you feel worthy and abundant, you generate wealth.

- It's not all about what you want to get; it's about how you can give what you want to get. This is how the law of abundance goes. If you want to be happier, help people be happy. If you want to have more money, support people making more money. On the other side of this, true abundance is also determined by your capacity to receive. Let yourself receive.

- Big problems can be solved with small actions

- It's all about consistency. Do the small actions daily, and before you know it, you have changed your life.

- How you do one thing is how you do everything. Clean up the micro-actions in your life, and that will reflect on the macro level.

- Don't be afraid of the "No!"s or failures. Highly successful people only see opportunities for learning and growth. The more you are prepared to fail and hear the "No!", the more growth you will receive as a reward.

- Don't get bogged down on what you feel limited to do with your resources. It's not about resources; it's about resourcefulness. Get creative and ask for support from your network.

- Invest in your growth and development. The more you evolve, the more those you serve can evolve. Increase the value of your service by increasing the value of yourself.

- The universe responds to who we are being. Be the best you.

- We don't always get what we want, but we are always guided to where we need to be. Trust in the journey.

- Your happiness and fulfillment are not always found in a person, thing, place, or achievement. Happiness and fulfilment are an inside job.

- Focus on what you want and why you want it. Leave the "how" it will happen up to the universe. You don't have to orchestrate this part. Let yourself be surprised.

- You become your habits. choose them wisely.

Self-mastery Reflection Questions

- What is stale or stagnant in my life?

- What limiting beliefs or self-sabotaging behaviours are holding me back from what I truly want?
- What am I tolerating in life, what micro-actions in my day do I need to improve ?
- What would it feel to completely and utterly love and accept myself now, and all past versions of who I have been? Knowing every single part of me is worthy of being loved, no matter what, can I let that love in?
- What is my "fierce grace" moment, and what are the things I am grateful for learning from this experience?
- What is my new vision for my life?
- If I were free to walk the rest of my life doing, being, and creating the ideal experience of life, what would that look like? Be really specific.
- How would it feel if my dream visions were actually here now, at this moment?
- How would my future, ultra-successful version of myself behave, what are their daily habits or practices?
- How can I implement these behaviours into my present day, week, and month?
- What are my superpowers?\

Support

I would love to tell you that this will be a smooth ride (and I wish for you that it is), but life is life, and it can come with tests, triggers, emotions, blocks, ups, and downs. *"Ride on the ever-changing waves of life,"* as Jack Kornfield would say and enjoy the ride.

Find yourself your tribe of accepting and supportive beings. Be there for one another, support one another, and rise together.

Be compassionate towards yourself, and just keep on going, step by step, and day by day.

You absolutely can do this.

There might be people reading this who are drawn to work together, to be supported on this journey. My job is to hold the highest vision possible for your life, not to accept the limitations your old friend fear keeps trying to tell you to keep holding you back from living your highest vision. I am here to support your navigation when you dropped the road map and need to be redirected back on track. I am here to listen deeply to you, hold space, and be the most truthful person to you in your life. I am here to celebrate and rejoice in your victories and successes. I am here to support you in creating your own life vision.

You might also be curious as to who needs a coach. Not everybody needs a coach. Here are some examples of the people I work with:

- People who feel the desire to make the world a better place;
- People who want to share their experience to create a positive result in others or the world;
- People who dream of freedom (financial, time, expression);
- People who know what they want, know what to do, but for whatever reason, they are not doing what they know they need to do;

- People who know what they want, but they don't know what to do to get there.

If you do feel that intuition calls you to work together, I would love to support you on your journey. First, before we have that chat together, I find it useful for further reflection.

What in your world do you need to be different? What might feel different in your world if we work together? How ready are you to commit to transforming your life right now?

If you feel called, you might be interested in joining a retreat, online one on one soul-centered coaching or my online group soul-centered coaching. You can find my email below and we can arrange a free exploratory call. If not, I wish you so much success on your journey and I hope my reflections and exploration have been the catalyst you need to awaken your powerful life creator within.

So, whether our paths cross or not, always remember, **"Yes, I Can!"**

"You really are the master of your life, and the power lies within your very capable hands. The canvas is your life, and you are the artist. Now tell me what magic is ready to be created in your life?"
~ Louise Cameron Edlund

With love,

Louise Cameron Edlund

Call to Action

1. **Personal Growth** – what new insights into yourself and your purpose have you discovered from reading this chapter?

2. **New Results** – What else is possible for your life now that you are aware you have the power to consciously create your dreams and goals?

3. **Professional Application** – What actions can you take today, this week, and this month to develop yourself, career, or service to this world?

About the Author

Louise Cameron Edlund is a Scottish-born leader of positive change, currently living in Ibiza, Spain. She is serving on her soul mission to support people who feel called to serve deeply, creating positive change for themselves and those they wish to serve. She works with clients creating positive impacts on the world, from all over the world. People who are ready to be, do, give, have and become more than they ever knew possible.

Originally beginning her career as a physical therapist in professional sports and private practice, Louise always had a fascination for understanding the physiology, mechanics, healing, and optimisation of the body.

After her own healing crisis left her to process and work with the impact our emotions have on our health, healing, and quality of life, Louise began to explore the bridge of the body and mind connection. This would unknowingly lead her on a spiritual path, living in India to learn from her masters.

The more Louise learned about the connections between the body, emotions, and spirituality, the more she realised she had to learn. Her passion for learning led her to study yoga, meditation, mindfulness, life coaching, spirituality, breathwork, and bodywork.

She is the bridge where science meets the ancient mystics – a completely holistic approach to experiencing the best version of yourself and your life.

The realisation that every single part of your life is connected helped Louise discover her multidimensional formula for life optimisation. If you work on the inside, your outside world changes, by changing your daily actions that bring you better results. If you want a fulfilled and abundant life, it is important to work on your body, mind, heart (emotions), and soul (your unique gifts, talents, and purpose for being alive).

You really can be the master of your life, and the power lies within your very capable hands.

Name: Louise Cameron Edlund

Website: www.louisecameronedlund.com

E-mail: info@louisecameronedlund.com

Facebook:
https://www.facebook.com/louisecameronedlund/

Instagram: @louise.cameron.edlund

Services:
- Retreats
- Online One-On-One Coaching
- Online Group-Coaching
- Onsite Workshops
- Inspirational Speaker

Ideal Clients: Louise works with people who feel the desire to make the world a better place for themselves, those they love, and those they serve. If you feel ready to move beyond the limited, to unlock your full potential, and be guided to be, do, give, have, and become more than you ever thought possible, you could be a perfect match.

The Power of Rejection

Dr. Izdihar Jamil
Money Coach, USA

"Rejection is a blessing. It's just a correction towards your destined success."

~ Dr. Izdihar Jamil

The Unthinkable

If I told you that for six years my Ph.D. research was rejected, and then one day it was a *"Yes!"* and I was on stage presenting at the top conference in the world... would you believe me? I remembered saying to myself, *"What's the point of doing all this anymore?"* Whenever I submitted my work to the top conferences, they kept saying *"No"* and sent it back. There was always something that was wrong about it. I was given excuses like:

"The study is not well grounded."

"There needs to be more solid experimental framing."

"Much of the presentation of the results was anecdotal."

"Your work did not make a clear contribution."

"Concerns about the methodological or statistical approaches."

My colleagues told me that, "*It really is tough one!*" What I heard from that was that "*You're not going to make it!*" and "*You're not good enough!*" I started to blame the reviewers with many reasons and justifications. Well, if you've played the blame game before, you'll know that the person that loses that battle is you, right? So, you can imagine I was a bit of a "drama queen," but no matter how much drama I created, it did not serve me well.

Frustration crept in. I'm constantly doubting my ability to the point that I had to struggle to believe in myself. When you're being rejected over and over again, you still have to try to make sure there is some pride left in you. But when you've been rejected over and over and over again for six years, what is there left of you?

In 2008, I started my journey as a Ph.D. candidate at one of the top universities in the world in England under a prominent professor. I studied how children communicate around a digital tabletop. Just imagine a table-sized iPhone where multiple children can interact with each other at the same time! I wanted to challenge myself and did the study across three countries: the United Kingdom, India, and Finland. So, my work wasn't just on the computer science aspects of it; it was also a hybrid between education, culture, and communication. You can not only say my work was multi-dimensional; it was also complicated. "*What have I done? Why couldn't I choose something easy?*" I remembered asking myself.

But somehow, my little heart kept on saying, "*You can do this!*" Truly, this research was the epitome of my Ph.D. success because of the highly valued contribution it gives to the community. In my vision, I could see myself presenting my work on a stage at the top conference in the world. Crazy, right? Especially for someone who has had been consistently rejected because their work hadn't been considered good enough to be accepted.

After six years of "*No!*"s and rejection, my dream turned into a reality. They finally said, "*Yes!*" and I was on stage at the top conference in the world presenting my work with my colleague. I remembered feeling scared, and yet I felt joy and happiness. I made it happen! Even my kids were excited for me. Of course, it wouldn't have ever been possible without my amazing team, but I want you to know that a "*No!*" isn't the end. It can just be the beginning of amazing things in your life. You can see my presentation here:

https://youtu.be/y7jCr6RNXNk

So, if I told you that years later, embracing rejection as a blessing has helped me to create a successful online business...would you believe me? If I had given up after the first few "*No!*"s, I wouldn't have been able to build a successful business, become the #1 International Bestselling Author, featured on Fox TV, ABC, Business Innovators, and have amazing clients around the world. Life isn't just about unicorns and roses. It is how you use your dramas and rejections and turning them into power is what will make you be successful.

Well, my friends, read on, because you'll be surprised how my worst nightmare is now my greatest strength. I'm about the tell you the best story that you've ever heard!

The Conflict

I'm not going to lie. I'm constantly battling with thoughts like:

> *I don't think I'm good enough.*
>
> *I don't have enough skills and knowledge.*
>
> *I don't know what I'm doing.*
>
> *I don't think people are going to pay me that much.*
>
> *I'm not worthy of success and money.*
>
> *I'm such a loser.*

It's just like one of those songs on repeat. You know what I mean, right? At times it gets louder, and at times it's just a soft whisper in the background. Here's the truth: I'm probably going to have those thoughts throughout my whole life. But, do I choose to let them control me, or do I choose to be in control over them?

After my Ph.D. work was rejected for six years, I was almost at the breaking point, but it was those secrets and the key lessons that I learned going thought that period that has helped me build a successful online business. Now, I love helping entrepreneurs and coaches attract more clients and make sales every day in their business <u>without</u> ads, techy funnels, or a big following. Check out my website at:

www.izdiharjamil.com

If you only knew how many people rejected and said, "*No!*" to my business offers on a daily basis, you would laugh and say, "*No way!*" I want to share with you my secrets, the key strategies, and wisdom that I learned throughout those years so that you can use rejection as a powerful tool to lead you to the biggest successes in your life. So, when people say "*No!*" to you, rather than saying, "*I'm done!*", you can say, "*Yes, I Can Do It! I've got miracles coming my way.*"

Are you ready? Say "*Yes!*" and let me take you toward your path of success and wealth because you are <u>worthy</u> of success and money.

I believe in you!

Breakthroughs and Lessons Learned

What made rejection such a heavy and painful experience was the story that I associated with it. Whenever people said "*No!*" to me, I made it mean that, "*I'm not good enough*" or "*I'm not worthy.*" That's what was making it full of pain and suffering because I viewed it that I was stupid and a big fat failure.

When I looked at things objectively, what happened was just what happened. It doesn't mean anything. The only meaning it had was the meaning that I attached to it. So, when I started to detach my story from what actually happened, suddenly, I could feel a heavy weight lifted from me. I was responsible for creating those painful stories. If I was the one creating the stories, then I certainly have the power to delete them. I let go of the attachments that I have around rejection and just followed the process.

I learned that rejection is just a correction towards my destined success. That's right, rejection is just a correction – without invalidation. All I had to do was just tweak it and make it better. I remembered when I received the result of my last submission. It literally was an easy "Yes!" Why? Because of all the corrections and tweaking that I made that there was <u>no way</u> it was a "*No!*" anymore. They couldn't fault the work because it was so strong, which lead to an easy "*Yes!*"

It's the same in my business. When people said "*No*" to me, I kept refining my business offers to the point it was an easy "*Yes*" for them. Why? Because what I offered was <u>exactly</u> what they needed to solve their problems. In my #1 Bestseller Book, *13 Key Strategies to Make Money Fast in Business*, I shared how understanding the market is the <u>key</u> to making money in your business. You can read more about that here:

https://www.amazon.com/dp/B07Z2PYX91

The other big factor was that I had an amazing team around me that supported me and held me into account for the last 10 years of entrepreneurship. My family, coaches, friends, and colleagues kept me moving forward. Even when things got tough, they never left my side and kept on saying, "*You can do this!*"

Yes, I've invested thousands of dollars in learning their proven system, expertise, and knowledge, but it has helped me so much to create a profitable business. I'm now scaling my business to seven figures and beyond. (Hey! Anything is possible, right?) When you know someone is in your corner, rooting for you, supporting you, coaching you, and holding you into account, you know that success is your destiny. It is your duty, responsibility, and obligation.

I'm tying down several key factors that have helped me moving forward after the constant rejections. These are some of my biggest secrets, and when you start to apply them, you'll start to see opportunities coming your way:

1. Let go of any attachments and stories that you have around rejection. It is not serving or empowering you.

2. Listen to the feedback around the rejection. Make corrections and tweak it. <u>Focus</u> on making it <u>better</u>.

3. Create an amazing team that will support you and will hold you accountable no matter what. Teamwork will make the dream happen.

4. Never give up. Keep moving forward, no matter what. Believe that your success is waiting for you. You just have to be persistent enough to want it.

5. Create a followup system for your business. The fortune is in the followup. Statistically, only 3% are ready to buy from you, and 97% are not. So, if you don't have a followup system, you will lose that 97 % of the clients.

6. When you say that you're going to do something, honor that promise no matter what happens. When you honor yourself to the highest level and to the point that your word is law, amazing things start to happen in your life.

7. Keep making prayers to the Creator because He is the One who can help make things happen for you.

The Ordinary World

I grew up in Malaysia, a beautiful country full of culture and delicious food. My dad worked in IT, and my mom taught chemistry in a school. I have three amazing sisters – we often fight and drive each other crazy, but we are still sisters at the end of the day. I remember during Eid celebration, we would go back to my grandparents and meet up with my aunties, uncles, and cousins. It would be total chaos with over 30 family members, but it was one of my happiest memories growing up. Plus, we got to eat amazing Malaysian homemade food, way better than burgers and fries!

One of the biggest values that I learned growing up in Malaysia is that family and education are important. I graduated with a Ph.D. in computer science from one of the top universities in England. These are the core principles that I instill in my children now: family and education.

We were also taught to be respectful and kind to others no matter who they are. Malaysia is a multicultural country with Malays, Chinese, and Indians making up the majority of the population. At an early age, we were taught to integrate with one another and to treat each other equally. That's why today, I find that I can easily connect with anybody regardless of their background and culture.

In 2015, my husband, my two young kids, and I moved to America to pursue our American dream. It was one of the scariest moments of my life – moving to a new country, leaving my families behind, quitting my secure job to pursue this dream. There were so many unknowns. We didn't have any family in America, but we had faith in this being the best decision for our family's future.

The Drama

In America, my family was verbally abused and harassed. People threw shit onto my doorstep. I was called vicious names when I was out. I was harassed at the grocery store. I was sad all the time, and I didn't feel safe taking my family out for fear of something bad could happen. I thought that I had made a big mistake coming here.

Feeling like my world was crashing down, I felt hopeless and helpless. One night, I was reading a storybook to my children and felt like God spoke to me through the story. I vividly remembered the line *"Ask for His Help and Mercy during difficulty, and you will find ease!"* I kept reciting and believing in that line over and over again, and things started to shift for the better.

I stopped playing the "victim" and took charge of my life. Things got better and better. I felt that no other families should go through what I had gone through. I felt that I was meant to do good things to help families have the best possible future. I focused my mindset on the positive, and that truly helped to shift things, because what you focus on expands.

The Call to Action

One day my husband told me that, "*I bought a program from this coach so that you can work from anywhere in the world while enjoying the kids!*". The program was about how to become an online consultant and coach.

I spent a few months learning about how to become an online consultant and coach. One of the first things I did was to understand the market – the problems, the pains, the challenges – before proposing a solution to solve my prospective clients' problems. With 10 years of experience in entrepreneurship, I started my online business.

I use social media to help entrepreneurs, coaches, consultants, and business owners to attract more clients and make more sales every day in their business. I knew that entrepreneurs face three big challenges in their business:

✓ They want to attract clients every day without using websites, paid ads, techy funnels, or have a big following. Basically, they want to have leads and prospects coming to their business for free.

✓ They want to book strategy calls or appointments daily so that they can share information about their products and services.

✓ They want to convert and make consistent sales so they can have a thriving and sustainable business.

So, I created the "Attract 10 Clients Now Course" and offered it for FREE to Entrepreneurs and Coaches to help kickstart their client attraction. It's a 5-day free program where I teach the best strategies to attract clients without any ads spent or websites needed.

Of course, attracting clients isn't enough. You've got to be able to convert them to create the cashflow. So, my up-level program is called the Client Conversion System. In the system I teach Entrepreneurs and Coaches how to attract clients every day and convert them into paid clients consistently. I've designed it so that they can implement quickly and use effective social media strategies that will get the results without ads, websites, techy funnels, or a big following. You can find out more here:

https://www.izdiharjamil.com

Did people say *"No"* to me and my offer? Totally! Did I feel frustrated, disappointed, and unworthy? Absolutely! Rejection is part of the process. It's just a correction towards your destined success. Here's what I did to pick myself back up again when they said *"No"* to my offer:

1. I tell myself that it doesn't mean anything. The pain comes when you create an attachment/story to the event. I take my emotions out of the transaction.

2. I followed the process in my system and added those *"No"*-people into my Follow-Up structure. At one point, only 3% are ready to buy from you, and 97% aren't. So, if you don't have a strong follow-up system, you'll lose 97% of your possible sales.

3. I tweaked my offer and focused on getting better and better until they said, *"Yes!"* because I'm so <u>irresistible</u>!

4. I focus on giving people <u>value</u> and creating a relationship with them because <u>contacts</u> lead to more <u>contacts</u>.

5. I <u>consistently</u> moved forward every single day and <u>never</u> looked back.

The best part was seeing my amazing clients getting results. Liv got clients within 30 days in her new niche. Aprila nailed her biggest client. Audra attracted 40 clients with just one post. Stephen J. tripled his offer price and made multiple sales. Stephen P. consistently books calls every day and makes sales.

If you're serious about attracting more clients and make more sales in your business, come and join me in my 5 Day Attract 10 Clients Now Course for free here:

From all that experience, I wrote a book that rose to be the #1 International Bestseller called *13 Key Strategies to Make Money Fast in Business Without Ads or A Big Following*. You can check it out here:

https://www.amazon.com/dp/1697242979

The Growth and Brightness of The Future

It was a Sunday afternoon, and my son was selling popcorn at the store for his Boy Scout's troop for the first time. I didn't want to do it because it breaks my heart to see people saying "*No*" to my son. But he told me, "*Mommy, let's go!*"

Being a newbie at popcorn sales, I saw him being fearless in approaching strangers. He had multiple "No"s, but he just brushed them off like they were not a big deal. He kept on asking, "*Excuse me, would you like to buy a bag of popcorn to help out the Boy Scouts?*" until he got a "*Yes.*" In one hour, from both popcorn sales and donations, he made $85!

My son taught me a beautiful lesson that it's not a big deal when people say "*No*" to you. Just pick yourself back up and repeat your efforts again and again, because the "*Yes!*" is inevitable.

Since then, I've created many amazing programs to help people make and keep money. I love seeing my clients being successful and looking forward to the best possible future for them. Some of my programs that have helped many people around the world are:

• **Client Conversion System.** Helping entrepreneurs and coaches to attract clients daily and consistently convert leads into paid clients.

- **Attract 10 Clients Now.** Helping entrepreneurs and coaches to attract clients daily using the fastest social media strategies.

- **A Sale A Day System.** Helping entrepreneurs and business owners make sales every day <u>without</u> ads, techy funnels, or a big following.

- **6 Figure Savings System.** Helping people save money with consistency and predictability.

- **VIP Business Scaling.** Helping entrepreneurs scale their business to six figures.

- **Bestselling Author.** Helping people to become <u>bestselling</u> authors in 90 days and raise their credibility.

- **Media Feature.** Helping entrepreneurs to be featured in the top media and be invited to TV appearances and speaking gigs, including *TED Talk*.

If you want to find out more about my work, just email me at:

izdihar@asaleaday.com

...and we'll have a chat, or connect with me on *Facebook* at:

https://web.facebook.com/izdihar.jamil.1

I'm now scaling my business to seven figures and beyond. (Anything is possible, right?) I'm excited to be working on my next Bestseller Book *Money Makers: 21 Hacks to Attract Clients Every Day Without Ads*. I'm thrilled to be looking forward to participating in more speaking gigs, including *TED Talk*s, and helping millions of people make money in their business.

I'm also looking forward to spending more time with my

family, explore the world with my family, and continue to help entrepreneurs and coaches make more money in their businesses.

The Reward

I am so happy and thankful that I have the <u>freedom</u> to run a successful business online and hang out with my family. It's every mom's dream! With an online business, I can take my family to spend the summer in Malaysia and still be making money in my business. Geographic location doesn't matter to me. All I need is my phone, laptop, and Wi-Fi, and I'm good to go!

I was interviewed on Fox TV, talking about the solutions to help entrepreneurs make money in Malaysia. Check out my interview here:

https://www.fox4now.com/the-morning-blend/female-leaders-spotlight-with-izdihar.

I was featured on hundreds of media, including FOX, NBC, ABC, and Business Innovator. I was also interviewed by prominent podcasters around the world. I have two #1 International Bestselling Books:

She Made It Happen
http://www.lulu.com/content/paperback-book/she-made-it-happen/26046439

13 Key Strategies to Make Money Fast in Business
https://www.amazon.com/dp/1697242979

BuzzFeed announced that I was one of the "Top 8 Sales Experts to Follow In 2020."

I am so blessed and grateful that I'm able to take my family to amazing vacations around the world. We played in the snow in Palm Springs, had sushi in Japan, and went on a cruise in Malaysia. I hired a Ferrari for my husband's birthday, and the look on his face was priceless. He works so hard for our family and rarely gets to treat himself. So, I made his childhood dream of driving a Ferrari a reality. I went to Bali to attend the "Make Your First Million Female Entrepreneur Retreat."

I get to volunteer at my kids' school, attend my daughter's ballet recital, and be at my son's ice hockey games. Do I still get rejections in my business daily? Yes! But, if I had given up when people said "*No*" to me, I would not have been blessed with all of these amazing miracles.

Rejection is a blessing. It is an opportunity for you to access miracles in your life. So, embrace rejection as a positive thing, because the "*Yes!*" is just there waiting for you!

The Wisdom

Knowing what I know now about the secrets to my success:

1. Rejection is just a blessing showing the way to your greater promised success.

2. Create an awesome team to help you be successful.

3. Keep moving forward no matter what and be prepared to tweak things as you go along the way. Just focus on getting better and better.

4. Let go of any attachments to rejections. They are just part of the process. They're no big deal.

5. Trust in yourself and your abilities, because you can do this!

6. Follow up with the people that said "*No*" to you, because eventually, they'll say "*Yes!*"

"*Don't over-analyze it. Start before you feel ready!*"

~Dr. Izdihar Jamil

Love and blessings,

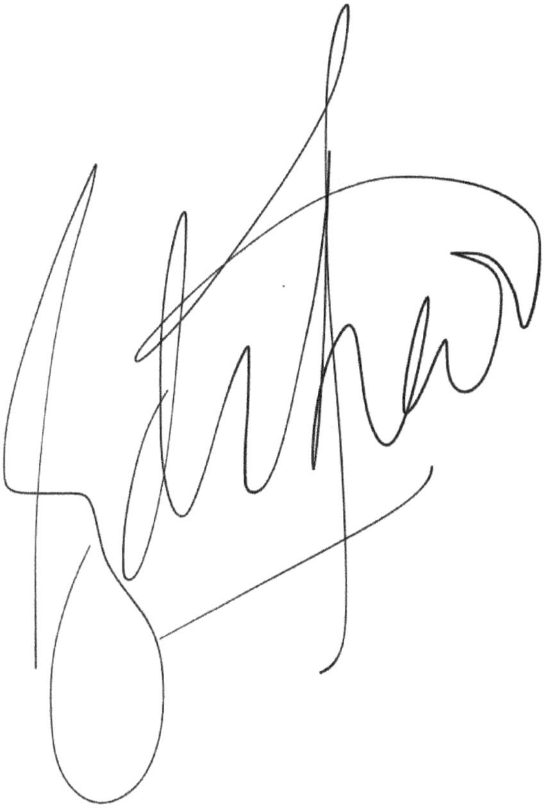

Power Summary

Let's do a quick recap so that you can grasp the key concepts:

1. Fill in the blank. Rejection is _____.

2. What did my son teach me about rejection when he was selling his popcorn?

3. What's the one thing that you need to implement after people said "*No*" to you?

Success Actions

Here are three success actions that you can take right now to make things happen in your business:

1. **30 Day Challenge**- Put up a post in social media every day in for 30 days and you will see a boost in your visibility and client attraction.

2. What's one thing that you can tweak to make things better in your life and business?

3. What's one positive thing that you can tell yourself today about rejection?

About the Author

Dr. Izdihar Jamil, Ph.D., is a Money Coach and Consultant who lives in California with her husband and children.

She loves helping entrepreneurs, business owners, and coaches to consistently attract clients and make more money using her proven system.

It is her greatest pleasure to see families living their best possible lives when they are able to make more money in their business.

Her methods are proven, simple, and effective – designed to produce the fastest results possible for her clients.

She is also the #1 International Bestselling Author with her books:

She Made It Happen
http://www.lulu.com/content/paperback-book/she-made-it-happen/26046439

13 Key Strategies to Make Money Fast in Business
https://www.amazon.com/dp/1697242979

In her spare time, she loves reading and baking for her family.

Business Name: Diamond Queen

Website: https://www.izdiharjamil.com

Email: izdihar@asaleaday.com

Facebook: https://web.facebook.com/izdihar.jamil.1

Instagram: @izdiharjamil

LinkedIn: https://www.linkedin.com/in/izdihar-jamil-ph-d-97236598

Products/Services:

- **Client Conversion System.** Helping entrepreneurs and coaches to attract clients daily and consistently convert leads into paid clients.

- **Attract 10 Clients Now.** Helping entrepreneurs and coaches to attract clients daily using the fastest social media strategies.

- **A Sale A Day System.** Helping entrepreneurs and business owners make sales every day <u>without</u> ads, techy funnels, or a big following.

- **6 Figure Savings System.** Helping people save money

with consistency and predictability.

- **VIP Business Scaling.** Helping entrepreneurs scale their business to six figures.

- **Bestselling Author.** Helping people to become <u>bestselling</u> authors in 90 days and raise their credibility.

- **Media Feature.** Helping entrepreneurs to be featured in the top media and be invited to TV appearances and speaking gigs, including *TED Talk*.

Ideal clients: Entrepreneurs, coaches, consultants and business owners

The Power of Clarity

Who Are You When Nobody is Looking?

Bayo Ao
Fast Growth Coach, USA

"Those in your life who don't have the clarity, determination, or courage to follow their own dreams will often find creative ways to discourage your dreams. Live your life based on your truth and never, ever let anyone or anything get in your way."

~ Bayo Ao

Failure x3 – Not the Best Way to Start, Is It?

When I went into business for myself, I didn't have any knowledge or experience of running a business or being my own boss. But what I did have was a feeling deep down on the inside that I was made for great things in life, and I could no longer bear the agony of knowing I could do, be, and have more if only I had the courage to take the first step and quit my job.

That's what I did in that summer in June, and I've never looked back, not once. When you decide that your dream is worth following, you're starting to take control of control of your future just like I did.

Most Fail Within Five Years!

Leaving a job that pays you every two weeks like clockwork and going into business for yourself can be a scary thing.
To this day, I remember reading the stats and being told this:
"Most small businesses fail within the first three years, and in five years, only 10% are still operating."

This is not what you want to hear from people whose opinion you respect or those who are supposed to be sources of small business success information.

It's interesting that one part of you yearns to be more and do more with your life, while another part of you, a part that wants to keep you safe, brings up and points out to you literally every piece of negative data that highlights things that potentially could happen to you if things don't work out.

For many people, that's the voice in their head that they choose to listen to. If that's you, I want you to know that it's not your fault. It's how we're trained to think and behave. It's a natural survival instinct that plays a role in what we do – or don't do – in life.

When the voice of caution is louder than the voice of determination, we stay put.

Often, we stay "stuck" in the status quo.

After all, if you've got a job that someone has decided you're worth paying a certain amount every two or four weeks, why would you leave that to step into an uncertain future, right?

Wrong, and here's why…

The Breakthrough and Lessons Learned

Did I feel afraid and fearful?

You bet I did, but it was knowing that I was making a choice that, if things turned out right, I'd look back over my life in the months and years to come and feel proud of my achievements.

On the other hand, if I didn't make the move to be in control of my destiny, I would have no one else to blame but myself, and that was something I knew deep down on the inside wouldn't be pleasant.

So, the choice was clear. I had to bet on myself, forge ahead, and give it my best shot.

Success wasn't guaranteed; however, failure, if it did happen, would be a great teacher, and I would learn valuable life lessons.

Five years into starting out on my own as a freelancer and three failures later, I knew this is what I truly wanted to do – be my own boss and change lives through teaching, coaching, and consulting.

A Tale of Two Worlds

I was born in London and went to live in Nigeria during a time when many immigrants decided they wanted to contribute to the growth of their homeland.

It was quite a culture shock for a young kid from East London.

The school system was different, and the people were different. Everything was different, and at the same time, very interesting compared to the world I knew up to that point.

I loved 7-Up soda because the bottle just seemed so big, and when we went to visit our grandad, we were spoiled with as many soda drinks as we wanted. The people were hard to understand because they spoke, at least to me at the time, in a "different way" from the cockney we were used to.

But that was the least of my challenges because there was school, and I did not fit in because I missed what I knew as the school system, the playground, the friends.

The Drama

My dad had to take on several jobs to make sure we had the things we needed, and one of those jobs meant he was away from home quite a bit. That was another strange thing for a kid living in a close-knit, very nuclear family in London.

Where was dad? And why was he away for so long?

All I was told was that he was working at his job. Maybe that sowed the seed in my tender mind that having a "job" wasn't necessarily something "nice!"

The Turning Point

I can't remember when exactly when it started, but my parents started arguing more and more, and I could tell it was about work.

I was right; the demands of my dad's job were starting to take a toll on my mum and my brothers and me. I remember that some other issues with relatives also started coming up at the time.

The only way we knew was because our uncles and aunts stopped coming around to our house, and we hardly got to see our cousins whom we used to see most weekends.

This "job" thing, I remember thinking to myself, wasn't something good if this is what it caused.

My mum started her own business, and so we got to see her less too. Our routine became so different that my brothers and I started yearning to go back to London, the place we knew as "home."

But we knew that changes weren't going to happen.

This was it for now.

The Turning Point

Things came to a head when my dad came home one day and told our mum that he quit his job and was going to start his own business.

I remember them having a big row about it, and secretly I felt glad ... because in my mind it meant we'd get to see dad more 😊

And so, he went ahead and started not just one business, but quite a few.

The icing on the cake for me was when my dad asked me to help him out in some of his businesses, and I got to learn a lot about entrepreneurship first-hand. I wasn't the oldest or the youngest, and I had no idea that those events were sowing the seeds for the life-changing decision I would make in the future.

The significance of him choosing me out of all his children was, in my mind now that I look back, a Divine Act meant to set me up for my future as an expert entrepreneur, global consultant to Fortune 500 companies, coach, and service-business owners.

Fast forward almost twenty years, I too stepped out and stepped up to become my own boss, but at the time couldn't really make the connection. I believe that who and what we are destined to become chooses us, but we need to be attentive to the signs, listen to our intuition, and heed the call.

The Downfall

These days when I teach, coach, and mentor, I often make reference to my three failures in business in my first five years. I do this not to discourage anyone but to encourage them and prepare them for the times ahead.

Understanding that failure is as part of the process on the way to success is something significant you need to know exists when you're in the process of heeding your own call to greatness.

I can't imagine what I would be doing today if I hadn't been attentive, listened, and, more importantly, responded to what the universe was telling me through that small voice within.

Do you feel your call to greatness is speaking to you right now?

Do you feel you're supposed to be, do, and have more than your current situation?

If you do, then that's your calling trying to get through to you.

You might be fearful or unsure about what to do, and that's okay. I lost count of the number of times I questioned whether I was on the right path and whether I'd made the right decision to start my own thing.

I did, and so will you too.

What it Takes

There are so many lessons we learn as we go through life. Each day presents itself with new challenges and new opportunities.

Some days it seems like all the stars are aligned, and everything works in your favor. Other days, not so much, and you might feel like the world is just out of alignment with itself, and you just happen to be caught up in the confusion.

When you decide to take control of your destiny, this isn't going to magically disappear, but with clarity, you'll not only pull through, you'll excel.

Clarity and action are the two main ingredients to be, do,

and have the things you truly desire and aspire for in life.

CLARITY

Another word for clarity is "clearness." When you have clarity in any situation, you're able to see what really is going on.

But if you don't feel clear about something or, in this case, how to move forward with the things you desire and aspire to, I want you to know that you're not alone.

There's an old saying:

"We suffer more in imagination than in reality."

~ Seneca.

This is to say that whenever we're facing or going through challenges in life, it feels like we're alone, but we're not.

Here's something worth knowing.

It's people that don't step up and take control of the key areas of life such as their relationships, their health and wellness, their finances, their career or business, their spirituality, etc., that <u>seem</u> to have it easy – but that's only on the surface.

Deep down on the inside, we all want to feel fulfilled and that we're living a meaningful life, and the way to do that is to be clear about what it is that you desire out of life, and then act to materialize those things.

Growth – A By-Product of Clarity and Action

Although I've focused mainly here on sharing my experience related to my decision to be my own boss, the lessons apply to all areas of life.

When you have clarity, and you act, you <u>will</u> grow during the process.

Choose anything you aspire to achieve, whether it's

related to your career, business, or other things you spend your time engaged in, as you're transitioning from where you are to where you want to be, you'll experience growth.

What I discovered as I've progressed along my journey from employee to service-business owner, coach, consultant, and more is that by association, you'll drop negative attitudes, weaknesses, and other attributes that don't now or no longer serve you.

The good news (or should that be the "great news?") is that you'll pick up skills, knowledge, perspectives, expertise, wisdom, and more that'll help you get what you want while you're serving others.

I know of no other situation that provides us with such a great opportunity in life, and it all starts with the decision to get clear about what exactly it is that <u>you</u> want out of life.

But it doesn't end there.

The other side of the coin is something you must know before you move forward.

What Are You Going to Give to the World?

You've probably heard the statement that "*Life is about give and take.*"

It is, and the more you're able to give, the more you're able to get.

I think it was the late Zig Ziglar, the American author, salesman, and motivational speaker who once said, "*You will get all you want in life if you help enough other people get what they want.*"

It's true, and I know this because my story reflects what happens when you have clarity and act in the direction of your dreams.

Remember, I'm from very humble beginnings and started as a totally unknown, independent freelancer who didn't even know the basics of running a real business!

Add to that the following:

- Even though I'm British, I'm of African heritage and I started at a time when the mention of "Nigeria" was synonymous with distrust. Not exactly great when you're trying to establish yourself as a trusted independent freelancer!

- I had zero connections when I started out — not even one.

- I didn't have a network and still to this day don't (I'm highly introverted, so that's not surprising, is it?).

- When I started out, I offered a commodity, i.e. teaching Microsoft Office skills to anyone who would hire me, and there were hundreds if not thousands doing the same thing who had been doing it for much longer than I had.

And what has clarity, action, and focus produced?

Here are just some of the things I believe are true blessings in my life:

- I've changed and continue to change lives through sharing my knowledge, wisdom, experience, and expertise with others.

- I've become a globally recognized business consultant, business coach, and knowledge expert.

- My clients include the largest household and brand names who are among the world's industry leaders at what they do.

You can do this and more I guarantee it, and it starts with clarity and action.

This is the power of clarity, and if you have the desire and truly aspire, you can be, do, and have anything you want in life personally or professionally.

My question to you is, do you have the clarity, and are you ready to act now?

The Payback

Have you noticed that the people who seem to be doing well and seem to have it all seem to attract things into their life somehow?

Most celebrities and popular people in our world that we know of, just seem to have this way of magnetizing good things to themselves.

It's about payback.

Every single one of the people you see today that you consider to be successful all started somewhere. Sure, there are some of them that were born with the proverbial silver spoon in their mouth. They may have had rich parents, relatives, or something else might be considered as the advantage they had, but even starting from that, a new position in life might cause that advantage to be lost if they didn't get clear and act to move in the right direction.

All I knew for a long time was that I wanted to change lives. Whether it was through teaching (which is where it all started), writing, or anything in between, I knew there was more to life than what I was experiencing at the time.

Making more money in a week than I used to make in a month doing what I loved and was passionate about, having an easy life, traveling the world in business class as part of normal work – none of that even occurred to me at the time. However, that and a lot more is part of the payback when you're giving to the life of others, and it starts with those two things – clarity and action.

Remember, as Zig Ziglar said, "*You* will *get all you want in life if you help enough other people get what they want,*" and it isn't hard to give if you're really committed to giving.

But Wait, There's More!

Some ads out here in the US are really amusing.

After the pitch person has gone through all the features and benefits of the product they're promoting, and you think they're at the end, they hit viewers with the line *"...but wait, there's more!!!"*

So, here it is...

I would be doing you a disservice if I failed to mention that what you've read here today is just one example of what's possible when you start where you are right now, with whatever you believe you <u>do</u> or you <u>don't</u> have you in your life.

You can't wait for perfection, because it doesn't exist.

I've remained highly introverted to this day. I probably can't change that because I consider it to be the <u>authentic</u> me. It's who I am in terms of my preference for dealing with the world around me and the people in it.

But here's the interesting thing...

You don't need to change who <u>you</u> are in order to create and live the life you desire. In fact, if you did that, you'd be "faking it 'till you make it," which is unethical and something you probably won't be able to sustain for any amount of time.

Can you imagine the embarrassment (if you took this route) and people discover that you're nothing like who you're pretending to be?

It happens all the time, and in these digital times we live in where everyone seems to be connected to others in our circle of real friends (or fake, social media "friends") and other communities people we know, the news will travel in no time at all.

So, don't even try to do it.

The person you are at your core is who people want to connect with. They don't want a "manufactured version" of you. They want <u>you</u> – quirks and all. They want the imperfect <u>you</u> so they can believe in themselves too, and it all starts with <u>clarity</u> about who <u>you</u> are when nobody is looking.

Takeaways – And a Warning about the "Law of Diminishing Returns"

Thanks for taking the time to invest in yourself by allowing me to take you on my journey of self-discovery and share inspiring moments from my life and from the lives of those I've been blessed to learn from, teach, coach and mentor.

I sincerely hope it inspires you; that it gives you hope and ideas on how to be the authentic <u>you</u> that you are when nobody is looking. I hope you're feeling inspired to take steps to be, do, and have those things that'll make your heart sing every day.

Let me leave you with some advice for the next steps to put this information into action in your life to achieve whatever you desire to achieve. It's a simple process and works for anything imaginable.

You won't find a successful person on the planet that doesn't use this system.

Here are the steps...

...but before that, let me share the "secret sauce" behind this method.

It's simple.
All you need to do is in your control.
You need to act on this information within 72 hours.
That's it.
For you to be successful with this system, you <u>must</u> act on it within the next 72 hours.
Why 72 hours?
I'll tell you...

It's because of something known as the "Law of Diminishing Returns."

That law states that when we determine we want to do something, if we don't act immediately, the more time we let elapse before we do act, the less likely we are to ever follow through.

So, for each of these steps, act on them ASAP, or at the most, within 72 hours to increase your chance of getting the results you want through following this system.

Can you do that?

Do _you_ believe _you_ are worth it even if it's not how you _"normally"_ do things?

If you can, then you've got this!

So, here are the ten steps to your success:

1. What do you want to be, do, or have? Just choose one thing to start with and get clear about it.

2. Find yourself an accountability partner, i.e., someone to hold you accountable for taking action on each step below.

3. Determine the information you're going to need to move forward.

4. Find that information.

5. Take the very first step immediately.

6. Follow through on each step.

7. Give some time to see the results you're seeking.

8. Check your results.

9. Correct anything that you need to correct.

10. Keep moving and keep checking your results to make adjustments where needed.

To succeed and achieve the things we want in life is

easy when we want it badly enough to do the things we need to do...consistently

~ Bayo AO

Bayo Ao

About the Author

Baya Ao is an entrepreneur and a coach that is passionate about helping others. He is the founder of "Courses that Change Lives." He offers courses that can help people be successful in their business and career.

He travels around the world for his work and lives in America with his family.

Founder: **Courses That Change Lives**

Website: https://coursesthatchangelives.com

Facebook: https://www.facebook.com/bayoao

Passion to Profits

Bryan Chamberland
Entrepreneur, Canada

"Ignite passion into your profession so you can drive purpose-driven success."

~ Bryan Chamberland

The Ordinary World

My name is Bryan Chamberland.

Walk with me through this chapter as I show you the secret to how turned my passions into my profession, while driving purpose into success using my skill sets & my story.

I'm also going to show you some practical ways to do more of the things you love with the people you love most using a simple framework at the end of this chapter.

Let's get right into it.

I grew up in St. Paul, a small-town in northern Alberta, Canada two hours northeast of Edmonton. We're kind of out of this world with our staple UFO landing pad, our UFO, a UFO pizza place, and there must be something in the water because country music stars like Brett Kissel, NHL hockey players like Kyle Brodziak, and golf pros like Jamie Sadlowsky seem to keep popping up out of our little farm town.

I grew up surrounded by a lot of love and support. The community was and still is incredible, but I struggled in school. I was diagnosed with a few labels growing up, starting with Asperger's syndrome early on, which is a high-functioning form of autism. I wrestled with trying to figure out how to navigate through all the feelings and frustrations associated with this insatiable desire for some kind of perfect pattern, while not having any control over any of it. Being an emotional guy who was uncomfortable in his own skin, I had no idea that these emotions and desires would turn into a creative strength later in life. As a matter of fact, I grew up believing I wouldn't amount to anything as teachers told my parents, right in front of me, to not expect much of yours truly. I guess they were wrong, thank God.

The Key Ingredients

There are 3 P's to your Perpetual Success – Passion, Profession, and Purpose. I'm going to break down these success secrets so you can start implementing them in your life and business.

P #1 – Passion

I continued to struggle well into my teens, but I found an attachment to music. I felt inspired by the guitar, and I spent hours listening to top-twenty countdowns while practicing improvisation over the hottest Songs using simple scales, shapes, and patterns. I connected with other musicians along the way, entered a few contests, like the "Battle of the Bands," and experienced a few wins early on. I got to play on the same bill as some of my favourite artists, and in the process, it all went to my head. I got lost in drugs, alcohol, and sex. I kept falling deeper into these vices, and as my problems kept getting bigger, so did I. I was addicted to food, porn – anything and everything damaging became my escape.

I was admitted into the hospital three times for drug- and alcohol-induced psychosis, and on my third stay at the Alberta Hospital psych ward, I told myself, "*Never again!*" I wasn't coming back – not like this, and not to this. I drew pictures of what I wanted to look like and wrote down the most audacious goals I could think of at the time.

Fast forward...

I'm out of the hospital, but I'm still struggling. I needed help. I've got no control over what's happening inside and outside at the time. I'm overweight; my hands and feet went numb one day; I was sick and scared. I went to my doctor for help. After a few tests, he came back to share that I was hypertensive, with high blood pressure and high cholesterol. He said if he was to put my liver next to a 65-year-old man's, it would look the same. I was 21 on the outside but 65 on the inside. But he also told me that it's not over, that the liver is a miraculous organ that can heal itself if you make the right decisions. I asked what I should do next. He said it's simple, start moving. Look at healthier alternatives with food. He said there's plenty of information online, and that if I wanted to see a change, I would have to let go of my drug and drinking habits.

So, I went home and took a good, hard look at myself in the mirror. You see, the mirror doesn't lie, and you can't lie to yourself while looking into your own eyes.

I cried out to God. I didn't hear Morgan Freeman from the sky or anything like that, but I did get peace and clarity at that moment. The next steps were simple – delete all 500 phone numbers from my phone and get a new phone number. No calls going out, none coming in, and start over. I did that. I quit drugs; I quit drinking and directed that energy to the gym.

I lost roughly 100 lbs. within six months of making the decision to change. I then studied kinetics and nutrition, became a personal trainer, then a head trainer at one of Edmonton's largest gyms within the year. I was featured in a magazine and found myself responsible for things I never thought possible. I was enrolled in a few sales and marketing courses within the company, and after about a year in the position, it occurred to me that I could apply what I learned to my love of music. I thought to myself, "*How hard could it be?*"

The idea expanded quickly, and suddenly, I started taking audacious action yet again. I downsized to being able to fit my clothes and most of my belongings, outside my instruments, into a little blue bag. I joke about how I used to live in a van down by the river while singing for my supper. I couch surfed & played to a lot of bar tenders.

P #2 - Profession

In the beginning of my music career I had this dream to play in front of thousands like most musicians. I thought if I were good enough, people would begin to do everything for me. I thought for sure I'd find a manager that would book all my gigs so you could hold my beer while I kiss your girlfriend kind of thing. How incredibly quickly I learned that this wasn't the case. Mostly because there were many other players out there that could play circles around me. There were way better performers that understood how to market themselves. And so, the marketing journey continued.

I applied what I learned from the marketing classes I was enrolled in while being a head trainer and started associating with some great producers in both the audio and visual space. I developed skill sets that helped me differentiate myself from the crowd. I started to organize and produce successful, online crowdfunding campaigns through a system called "Pledge Music." I did enough to garner attention from top-20 artists and a *Canadian Idol* judge. This allowed me to tour and play with some of the best in their respective fields and genres in the country and mainstream rock space.

Fast forward…

I'm suddenly working with an award-winning establishment touring all over North America on a million-dollar tour bus, sharing my skill set and my story with a mission to uplift and empower youth using music as the vehicle.

I spent roughly two and a half years with this group on tour, and it marks the biggest developments of my life. Within this time, I was married and became a dad. A month into my first son being born, it all came crashing down. I went from living the dream touring with the best of the best in multiple areas of expertise from marketing, content development, presentation, storytelling, audiovisual, design – you name it – to losing my dream job.

When I was let go, I played the blame game, but it didn't help anyone or anything. When I started to take responsibility for my life in the face my fear, things started to shift. It wasn't the greatest feeling in the world, but I owned up to my mistakes and learned a lot. I would even go ahead and say it was one of the best things that happened to me even though it didn't feel like it at the time.

Even with knowing that taking responsibility was the right thing to do, I wrestled to realign my passions with my profession again. It felt like I was jumping from one thing to the next. I felt like I just kept quitting, but deep down, I knew I wasn't a quitter. There were reasons for the seasons. I kept looking for my purpose not realizing that I was living it out through the process. I needed my pain to get to today. It was extremely humbling, and there are still off-days, but it all makes sense, nothing was wasted.

Every course, every certificate, every long night studying, waking up early to dig deeper to find that next element, every time I stopped one venture to start another– it wasn't quitting. It was developing the bigger picture to bring it all together. From the micro-perspective, it sucked. I didn't understand it. But from the macro-perspective, it was necessary. The right people were placed in my path, and I was able to realign my passions with my profession and found that my purpose was never gone.

That's the secret to aligning your passion with your profession and your profession with your purpose. Realize your purpose is always there.

As you can see, I've experienced it all. I've experienced

amazing highs, and I've lived through incredible lows. I was able to build momentum and experience great successes; then I had to start all over from scratch. Now I'm writing this to you today, and I'm an Owner, Digital Strategist, High-Performance Coach, Speaker and Writer.

P #3 - Purpose

What's the secret sauce? Why was I able to accomplish a level of success most spend a lifetime striving to achieve not once, but twice after a massive blow that had the potential to cripple me and leave me bitter and angry?

I understood that driving purpose into success would ignite a sense of significance. I understood the importance of understanding and developing a "Why" for everything I wanted to accomplish and for the people I love most. Even more important was learning that there's two layers to a "Why" when it comes to back-engineering your goals. I also understood the next steps were to discover the "What" and the "How" with the "Why" in mind.

1. There's the "Why" to you and your immediate ecosystem – which for me is my family and our desire to live out our passions together while experiencing freedom doing the things we love with the people we love most.

2. Then there's your "Why" to the world – which for me is to echo Point #1 by helping others achieve the same thing resulting in more of Point #1.

3. The "What" are the products and services – which for me is our team's Marketing, Sales, and coaching courses that lead to our Ad Agency services along with our High-Ticket items and Multi Residual Stream

Systems.

4. The "How" are the delivery systems and strategies – which for us are online advertising and educating online, face to face and through events. If you ever want to learn more or inquire about working with my team and I, simply visit:

www.missionignition.marketing

… and setup a quick call or email:
hello@missionignition.marketing

The Turning Point

You'll notice I outlined above that my "Why" to the world is an echo of my "Why" to me. Why are both "Whys" a reflection of each other? I realized in order to fill a specific gap my life, the fastest way to achieve my desired outcome was to help others to do the same.

I had to learn that providing solutions was going to help me get to our destination faster than focusing on sales. The interesting part of what came with this lesson was learning that a sense of purpose would come with this as well, because relationships began to flourish, and as a result, I was able to uncover and understand what I call the Four Pillars of Wealth.

1. Time – The most valuable currency we have.
2. Health – Without it, our time is short.
3. Relationship – Without it, money means nothing, and without health, it's hard to maintain good relationships.
4. Cashflow – There are four quadrants to understand

in this point. My suggestion is to read Robert Kiyosaki's book, *Rich Dad Poor Dad*, and learn how to make your money work for you instead of trading time for dollars.

As a result of these findings, we've developed a few strong statements within our organization. These thoughts and statements are our "secret sauce" to staying on course and hitting targets. It's what has led to our wins and what continues to bring us more using a clear message that converts. My suggestion to you in finding and building your Perpetual Success is to take the time to develop the two layers of your "Why." By doing so, it will help you uncover your "What" and you "How."

Once you've gained some clarity on your "Why," "What," and "How," it's important to come up with your mission, vision, and values statements to help you stay the course.

Here are a few quick examples of our statements to the world that depict our Mission, Vision, and Values systems:

Mission
To help Entrepreneurs Ignite their brand so they can do more of the things they love with the people they love most.

Vision
To make freedom a common practice in the world by helping entrepreneurs turn their passion into profits.

Values
Relationship is the foundation of everything we do. People over profits, we will never let money stop us or drive us.

Tying it all in to one significant statement:

"We help you Ignite Passion into your Profession so you can Drive Purpose-Driven Success"

These statements encompass who we are and drive everything we do. I encourage you to come up with your own version(s) of these messages so that you can be fully invested in your dream, your vision, mission, and value system. They'll drive your success & significance deeper, wider, and faster as you live them out. They'll help you get more quality buy-ins with like-minded individuals driving perpetual purpose-driven success into your business, your mission, vision, and value system.

The Wisdom

If you're going through pain. I want so badly for you to understand that there's purpose in your pain if you declare it. Your pain can become your platform if you decide to embrace it. The entrepreneurial journey is messy. If you're in it solely for money, it'll either lead to burning bridges, burning out, or both.

The Brightness of The Future

I'm back in my element doing the things I love with the people I love most. My vision is to make freedom a common practice in the world by helping entrepreneurs turn their passion into profits because as you've read up to this point; I've struggled, I've felt alone, abandoned, shackled by limiting beliefs and I've been broke. My "Why" to my immediate ecosystem and myself is to experience more of the things I love with my family. My "Why" to the world is an echo of my "Why" to myself. I am passionate about helping people do more of the things they love with the people they love most, because I know the more people I help in this area, the more freedom my family and I will experience.

How is our mission being met? I am partnered with a full-service marketing firm, and I own and operate an ad agency with multiple, key, joint-venture partnerships around the world. My team and I help you Ignite Your Brand. We work with Entrepreneurs as well as small, medium & large businesses to create a clear message that converts while increasing their success through strategy. We do this with an aim to get you up & running with paid advertising & automation as quickly as possible so your business can work for you, instead of you getting lost in your business.

I am blessed to have the freedom to do the things I love with the people I love most while helping others do the same. We are also only just starting to scratch the surface of our mission, vision, and value system(s).

This is how you ignite passion into your profession while driving purpose-driven success.

I hope you found great value in this chapter.

All the best in health, wealth, and relationships always.

"Do more of the things you love with the people you love most."
~Bryan Chamberland

Power Summary

Let's do a quick recap so that you can grasp the key concepts:

1. What are the three Ps?

2. What are the four Pillars of Wealth?

3. What are the three important statements that you should create to help you stay on course?

Success Actions

Here are three success actions that you can take right now to make things happen in your business:

1. Find your "Why," your "What," and your "How."

2. Take a solutions-over-sales approach

3. Build long-standing collaborative relationships with like-minded people.

By doing these, you'll begin to live a life of purpose-driven success, doing more of the things you love with the people you love most.

About the Author

Bryan Chamberland is an Owner, Digital Strategist, Speaker, and Author from St. Paul, Alberta, Canada. He's overcome addiction, mental health challenges, and mass rejection. Bryan has gone from zero to touring all over North America with some of the best speakers, performers, and content creators of today. From the top of his game to having to start over from scratch, he's now hitting new heights with a vision to make freedom a common practice in the world by helping entrepreneurs turn their passion into profits; starting with marketing & sales strategies through automation while building longstanding collaborative relationships with like-minded individuals.

Bryan Chamberland

Business Name: Mission Ignition Marketing

Website: www.missionignition.marketing

Email: hello@missionignition.marketing

Products and Services: Marketing and Sales Coaching, Online Courses, Automation, and High Ticket Residual Systems

Ideal Clients: We work with Creative & Innovative Entrepreneurs. We help creative entrepreneurs build their own systems by creating a clear message that converts while increasing their success through digital strategy & automation. We also work with innovative Entrepreneurs by providing them with a proven winning high-ticket sales system.

Success is the Best Revenge

Chris Tauriello
Nutritionist and Fitness Chef, Canada

"Day by day, in every way, I am getting better and better."
~ Emile Coue

The Unthinkable

If I told you that I was once a heavy smoker and drinker and then transformed my life, would you believe me?

I was 14 years old when I had my first smoke. At the time, I was a good kid that was well-mannered and extremely active. I remember the first night I smoked so vividly. I went to a party that my parents didn't know about with seven friends to a park with a secret gate, close to where I grew up. We were meeting with some friends from another nearby high school.

The irony of it all is that while growing up, I really hated smoking. If fact, I contracted bronchitis due to smoke inhalation when I was 11, which affected my activity level and my confidence.

At the time of graduation, my friends started smoking, and because of peer pressure, I began to smoke. I never thought I would be a smoker or hang around a crowd that drank and partied. I became a product of my environment, as most kids do.

I always knew it was harmful, but that night at the park was a lot of fun. After that night, I was hooked, and smoking became an ingrained habit. Something I had previously abhorred became my escape from the boring reality of school and routine.

Fast forward seven years of hard smoking, drinking, and partying…

I was lying in a hospital bed, sick and overweight, and without a friend in the world. I was addicted to smoking and drinking. The Dr.'s looked at me but didn't say much; my family didn't say much either, but I could tell they were disappointed.

Smoking and drinking were a regular part of my life. I knew I had to change because my life depended on it. I wish someone had told me earlier that if I didn't kick the bad habits, I'd be lying in a hospital near death.

On the night of February 23rd, 2008, I decided to change my life forever.

At that pivotal moment, I made the decision to quit smoking and drinking for good and focus on improving my life. I knew I had to get healthy. At the time, I didn't know it, but I also wanted to share my story with the world, which is why I have started a health consulting business that I operate today.

I want to share this story with you because I want you to have a better life, avoid becoming sick, making the same mistakes I did, and focus on improving your health so that you can enjoy your life.

If I didn't make that choice on the night of February 23rd, 2008, I wouldn't be here telling you this. I wouldn't be married, and I wouldn't have my own business.

How many amazing things are awaiting you in life? Take the path back to health. This is your life.

I invite you to take a journey with me through my past to see how I transformed my life completely through sheer will and determination, a little help from loved ones, and my God-given ability to turn setbacks into momentum!

How would you like to lose 30 lbs. in three months while eating delicious food and without fad diets or dangerous diet pills?

How would you like to quit smoking and transform your life?

How about improving your mental health and cognitive ability through diet and lifestyle changes?

Yes, or yes? Read on...

This is the story of how I started my business. I hope you enjoy reading it.

Thank you!

The Conflict

I knew that it was inappropriate for me to be smoking. How is it okay for any 14-year-old to be smoking?! I felt lost and didn't know what I was doing. I didn't want to tell my parents because I knew they would be disappointed.

Things just kept getting worse.

A few months after I started smoking, I also started drinking. It tasted like shit, but I did it anyways because I thought it was cool and my friends were doing it. This may sound funny now, but we often stole from my parents' stash of alcohol. It wasn't right, but I wanted to make an impression.

I was always in trouble and didn't do well at school, although most of my teachers liked me and thought I had a lot of potential.

On the night of February 23rd, after seven years of smoking, I knew enough was enough, and I quit for good.

The Breakthrough and Lessons I've Learned

The 23rd of February is a monumental day for me. Each year I celebrate in good health because that is the commemorative day that I decided to get clean and transform my life through food, nutrition, and fitness.

I knew I had had enough and wanted a healthier life, a healthier me. It was a scary time, but I knew I wanted to reach my full potential, even if just for revenge – against life and the world, and against my friends.

I now realize that my circumstances were based on my life's decisions, and part of what I now teach my clients is based on deeply rooted habits and behaviors.

I went cold turkey, and I let go of the past. It wasn't easy because I had lost all my friends and had been smoking and drinking for so long. But even then, I knew it was the right choice. I had made the decision to improve my life and show everyone that I was more than just the kid who was broke, sick, and nearly dead.

After all the mistakes and crazy things I had done, I learned to have faith in myself and trust in my own abilities. When you make a decision, opportunities suddenly come your way, Unknown to me, my uncle got me a subscription to *Men's Health* magazine, and it sparked a passion within me. I started doing research on health and wellness programs.

As a result of that original spark, I trained to become a fitness coach, then a chef, and now a nutritionist. I help people to improve their mental health, lose weight, and reach their full potential. You can find me on my site at:

www.tauronutrition.com

The Ordinary World

I grew up in a wonderful neighbourhood with a loving and supportive family. My parents, siblings, and entire family were very involved. They meant well and had the best intentions for me.

I was super-active as a kid, spending my days running around and playing sports. Getting the right amount of exercise was hardly ever an issue. I grew up in an Italian family where we had tons of food, and it all tasted so good. Even though I was very active, I had a belly for most of my teenage years, and that affected my confidence.

I think for most families growing up in the Western world, we're subjected to a lot of processed food in the supermarkets and in advertisements. I'm not saying don't enjoy yourself because that is important too, of course, but that we would be a lot healthier as a race and culture if we didn't regularly eat processed junk.

Through my experiences, I now know that is my message.

The other thing I find important that has taught me a

valuable lesson is being the change I want to see in the world. My avenue of expression is health, so I'm routinely learning and implementing new strategies to ensure I practice the best principles and preach the very same.

I think it speaks to you, my audience, and shows that I'm living a well-rounded life instead of being a hypocrite. I'd hate that and think you wouldn't listen if that were the case. I've created this business to help you to lose weight, quit smoking, and live a healthier life, but also to share my vision and experiences with the world to help you improve your health. I love creating recipes and exercise plans for my clients. Part of what I offer also includes 1-on-1 consulting.

One of my entrepreneurial clients loved the menu I created for her and her family. The recipes are simple, fast, healthy, and delicious. Anyone can create them with ease.

You will find that to be true.

The Turning Point

After I escaped that chapter of my life, I felt compelled to start over – to mature and grow up. I cut out all those friends, started working out, cooking for myself, and eating healthier. One of my favorite recipes that I used to make was beef and broccoli. It served as a good starting point and is very tasty. I've now updated that to tempeh and broccoli.

Recipe: Easy Tempeh and Broccoli.

Yields two-four servings

Ingredients:

- ¼ cup wheat-free Tamari
- 1 shallot, diced
- 1 tbsp garlic, minced
- 2 lbs./900g tempeh, bite-size cubes
- 1 tbsp. sesame oil
- 2 tbsp. rice vinegar
- 1 tbsp ginger, minced
- 4 cups broccoli florets

Method:

1. Bring a cup of water to boil.

2. Heat a small amount of tamari in a large rondeau or sauté pan, add the onions and garlic. Sauté for 2-5 minutes or until the onions are clear (this is called "sweating" the onions).

3. Add the tempeh and sauté, stirring gently, for about 5 minutes. Stir together the oil, vinegar, and ginger and add to the sauté.

4. Steam the broccoli in the boiling water with the lid on for about 3 minutes or until tender, but still *al dente* (tough to the bite). Add the broccoli to the tempeh mixture and keep warm

5. Serve and enjoy!

I started out doing simple things: making rice, doing pushups during commercials while watching TV, taking rest when I needed it most, and reading daily. I also enrolled in business school. I always wanted to have a business of my own. The uncle that helped me transform my life with the subscription to *Men's Health* magazine always told me to find financial freedom. My dad and grandfather were in business together for many years, and my rich uncle owned his own business. It seemed like a wise decision and became my driving passion.

Life seemed to be turning around for me. I was taking control of my life instead of playing the victim.

One day, my parents asked me to move out. I was shocked and scared, but it turned out to be one of the best decisions they ever made for me. I had to start fending for myself, and that meant actually working. I found various kitchen jobs around my new area and pretty soon had bought myself a car as I had always dreamed. I was managing pretty well.

The main thing is to continue to focus on the right things in life, the things that make you feel good. I learned that you have to keep moving forward in life.

My love for health and education lead me to attend a post-secondary school for fitness training. Shortly afterward, I also attended culinary school. That was the moment of my life that shaped me into who I am today.

The revenge then happened naturally…

The Call to Action

Just before I went to culinary school, I was working in a kitchen and had received concert tickets as part of a thank-you from a vendor. It was at that concert that I met someone who worked for the Ministry of Trades. She was also the childhood best friend of the performer we were watching. That inspired me to enroll in a culinary apprenticeship. From there, I landed a corporate job as a cook. I also met a beautiful girl who is now my wife.

Things were going well, yet, there was still thing aching desire to do more.

Everyone was so proud of me when I graduated from culinary school with honors. I had turned a day job into a career, although something was still not quite right. I was working five days and in school for two days each week. I had no time for myself and I knew that there had to be more to life. I took the hard way out of the industry. Instead of just quitting and getting another job, I enrolled in a nutrition course.

For two long years, I was super-busy again, but I felt like my life's purpose and I were realigning. At the end of the course, I had a hard decision to make: either keep my corporate job with steady pay and security and deny my life's purpose, or attempt the board exam, start a new career path, and leave the corporate world.

Key Ingredients

Twelve years since that fateful February 23rd, I lost my excess weight quickly – 30 lbs. in three months – just from what I learned at nutrition school, and I've managed to keep it off. I also have never touched a cigarette again, and only drink moderately on special occasions.

I am also now married, and we share the love of meal prep, food, and nutrition. I still exercise three to five times per week and enjoy light exercise and relaxation time with my wife and family.

Today I enjoy the fruits of my labour: I lost the weight, left the corporate world, started a new career, and now live a purpose-driven life. I am proud to say that I am now a certified nutritionist and I teach others what I have learned over the course of the past 12 years and how I lost my excess weight.

I have tailored my business to help you obtain an ideal weight, improve your mental health, eat healthy and delicious foods, all while exercising moderately and regularly and enjoying life to its fullest. I offer free, 45-minute strategy sessions where we discover your goals and how I can help you achieve them.

If you are serious about your health, book a free consultation with me. This is the link to my booking page:

www.tauronutrition.com/book-online.

I know I have a long way to go to achieve my lifelong dreams, and I'm okay with that. That's part of the journey and the growing process.

The Growth

I married my best friend on September 21st of 2019. I never thought that someone could love me so much. After years of heartache and bad relationships, I've found someone who loves me for me. We share a vision for our lives and the world through my Best Body Program.

I'm in the process of scaling up my business in 2020. I want to help 100 people this year reach their full health potential and get the best version of their body through 1-on-1 coaching and custom menu and exercise planning.

The Best Body Transformation Program is something I am creating to help you get into the best health possible. So much more is achievable when you work as a team, so I would recommend getting your partners involved in your health journey.

This program is the culmination of the past 12 years of my life experiences in health, food, and nutrition. There is nothing like it on the market today. I am so passionate about helping people to quit smoking and break addictions through diet and lifestyle so that they can be healthier and happier.

I am really excited to be working on this project as a best-selling author. My dream is to scale my business to six figures, get more speaking engagements, and spread my message to the world. If you're struggling like I was before, keep telling yourself, "Yes, I can!" My "why" was extremely powerful; I wanted to get revenge. It can serve you if you use it well.

I hope that you've been inspired by my story to start your own health transformation. My door is always open to you if you need help with your transformation journey.

The Wisdom

Knowing what I know now would have helped my 21-year-old self a great deal. Here is a shortlist of my secrets to success:

1. Opportunities will come to you when you make a choice to better yourself.
2. Even when you are scared, know that it is okay and that you will survive and become an even stronger person than before.
3. Live with purpose and enthusiasm.

"My dreams turn into goals then into reality
one day at a time."
~ Chris Tauriello

To your health and happiness,

Chris Tauriello

Power Summary

Here is a quick exercise to help you with learning:

a) I knew that smoking at 14 was a harmful decision, but I did it anyways. Can you relate?

b) When I started on my health journey, what was one of the first things that I did?

Success Actions

Try these three things to boost your health and wellness today:

1. Start small and keep it simple. Here is a quick 10-minute exercise that I do regularly to maintain my health:

   - Pullups/pull-downs: max reps/8-10 reps;
   - Dumbbell swings: 25-50 reps;
   - Pushups: max reps;
   - Jump squats: max reps;
   - Dips: max reps;
   - Hanging leg raises: max reps.

   (I often do two sets of each, and if I'm feeling really brave, I'll perform each exercise as part of a circuit, meaning back-to-back without any rest in between exercises. I also like to mix and match these exercises so that the routine is not in the same order and I keep from getting bored.)

2. Make a commitment to cook at least one time per week. Click here:

www.taurorecipes.com

…to get a sample of some quick recipes.

3. Schedule a free, 45-minute call with me so that I can help you set your health goals.

Book at this link:

www.tauronutrition.com/book-online.

About the Author

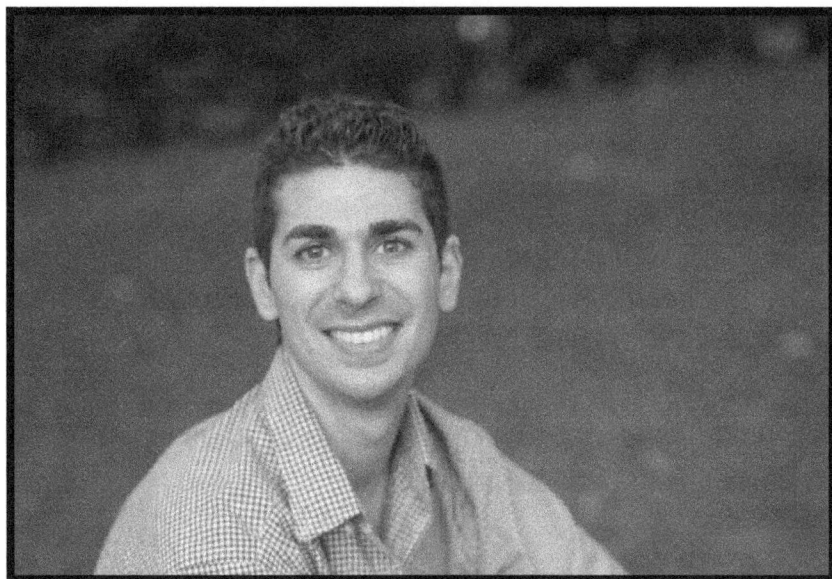

Hi, my name is **Chris Tauriello**. I am 32 years old, married, and am a certified nutritionist and chef. I have been on my own health journey for the better part of 10 years. I have graduated from personal trainer college, culinary school, and more recently, nutrition school.

When I was overweight in 2016 because I was too busy, I knew I'd find my way back to my ideal weight. I lost 30 lbs. in three months without bulky gym equipment, fad diets, or dangerous diet pills. I now show my clients how they can lose weight and overcome their mental health issues.

Business Name: Tauro Nutrition

Website: www.tauronutrition.com

Facebook and LinkedIn: Chris Tauriello

Products and Services:
- 7-day "Best Body Trial Program"
- 30-day "Best Body Custom Plan"
- 8-Week "Best Body Transformation Program" (under development)

Ideal Client: My ideal client is someone from an English-speaking country between the ages of 25 and 50 and is struggling with mental illness.

Always Trust and Believe in Yourself

Elle Hari
Twin Flame Alchemist, U.S.A

*"The Universe is not outside of you. Look inside yourself;
everything that you want, you already are."*

~ Rumi

WTF Was Wrong with Me???

Like most people experiencing a twin-flame journey, I first discovered that I had embarked on my twin-flame journey after it had already begun, and I was caught up in the throes of it.

The "throes" of a twin-flame journey vary in degree and intensity from person to person, but they usually consist of obsessive thoughts, heartbreak like no other, and a physical pain akin to what it surely must feel like to have your soul ripped from your body. That's the best way that I can describe it.

The kicker is that this all comes on the heels of the most intense, ecstatic feelings you could ever imagine feeling. It's a comedown and let down so great that you could feel like your entire world had suddenly been turned upside. Nothing makes sense anymore.

For me, the extent of all of the above culminated in me morphing into a helpless blob lying on the floor. It was too painful to get up and face life. I felt like a zombie…staggering helplessly through the dark abyss of a world that I no longer recognized nor wanted to be a part of.

I had no idea what had happened or why. All I knew was that I was flying high one minute and then writhing and crying out in pain on the ground the next. My natural inclination was to ask, "*What's wrong with me?*"

I spent the first six months in this seemingly endless abyss of pain searching for answers about what was going on with me and, more importantly, how I could fix it. I had consulted 13 different "experts" – from both spiritual practices and mental ones – but nothing resonated, nothing helped.

For the most part, I believe they were well-meaning. They simply had no clue what I was experiencing. (I mean, how could they when I didn't even know what it was, myself?)

They were all focusing on what was wrong with me – what I was doing, saying, thinking, and feeling that wasn't helping my physical situation. And, that's what I had been focused on, too – desperately hoping that every new day would bring the breakthrough, the relief, and the answers I needed to end my pain and heartbreak and be flying high once again.

I had been waiting six months for my salvation, which always seemed to elude me because I had (we all had) been approaching my dire situation from the complete opposite direction than was necessary.

As it turned out, nothing was wrong with me. Everything was a blessing and a gift.

Yes, even the pain.

When the Student Is Ready, the Teacher Will Appear

One particularly desperate day six months into my journey, I happened upon my teacher who not only saved my life by plucking me out of the black hole of misery I had existed in for half a year but also ended up providing me with the key to ultimate success in every aspect of life.

She did this by sharing divine truths with me, which, like all truths, are simple and just <u>feel</u> right. When you stumble upon divine truth, you'll <u>know</u> it. It feels good.

Here are a few examples of divine truth:

- You are your soul (not your mind).

- Your soul is a spark of source energy (the most powerful energy that exists).

- Your soul is limitless, boundless, fearless, omnipresent, timeless, all-powerful, all-knowing, miraculous, perfect, and pure love, peace, abundance, and bliss.

- Your soul is orchestrating everything in your life.

In other words, you <u>are</u> everything that you could ever want; in fact, you are so much <u>more</u> than that because your mind can't conceive of <u>all</u> that is.

The reason I wasn't feeling any better for six whole months is that I was trying to "fix" and "heal" myself. What my teacher taught me was that there was nothing to "fix" or "heal" regarding myself. I wasn't broken, sick or damaged. I am perfect.

The only reason we ever feel broken or damaged is when we are out of alignment with our non-judgy, accepting selves. When we feel lost, sad, hopeless, anxious, or simply "not good," it's because we are focusing on what is going on around us – outside of us – that we wish was different or we could change. Of course, this is futile. Any sense of control we have over other people and situations is an illusion.

Instead, and especially during times of distress, we need to turn our attention inward onto ourselves. We need to trust and believe in those divine truths I mentioned above, which equates to trusting and believing in ourselves.

Once I truly resonated with those truths, I automatically had full trust and belief in myself. I know now that, without any doubt, my soul is in charge of everything that comes into my life, and, because of that, everything is happening for a reason.

Everything is exactly the way it's meant to be in every moment because my soul and the Universe don't f*ck up. They are perfect; therefore, everything they create in my life is perfect, too.

Who is my mind to ever judge perfection?

We often hear people advise us to love ourselves, but they never quite tell you how to do that. What does "love yourself" mean?

All love, by definition, is unconditional. Loving yourself would be accepting yourself and all that you orchestrate without judgment. Attaining the space of acceptance without judgment only comes once you fully trust and believe in yourself.

So, ultimately, loving yourself comes down to trusting and believing in yourself.

Realizing My Purpose

Resonating with the divine truth is a process. It doesn't happen right away or overnight. It's not like you read it, commit it to memory, and try to apply it in your everyday life.

Divine truth far surpasses the mind. It's not about "knowing." It's about resonating. Resonance is remembrance. It occurs on the level of the soul. Your soul already knows the truth. Your soul is all-knowing, after all. In order to resonate with truth, you must shift closer into alignment with your soul and remember on the deepest soul level everything you already know.

This is where my teacher came in. She taught me how to energetically shift closer into alignment with my soul. This involves transmuting or alchemizing your mental (fear-based) energy into soul (love) energy. This process energetically lifts you out of the energetic field of the physical (fear-based) world and into the energetic field of the soul (love).

The more fear-based energy you alchemize into love, the more you gradually rise out of the fear-based, energetic matrix. This is what we refer to as the "ascension process."

As with all things soul-related, it takes a while to resonate with this concept. My resonance with it continues to expand as I move along my path towards ascension. It won't end until I reach full ascension, which will most likely not occur in this lifetime.

To get where I am now, I worked with my teacher every single day for two years. This required a total commitment from me of nearly every resource imaginable – my time, my energy, and my finances – and it was…

…scary!

The Universe and the soul working as they tend to do occurred right after my divorce and when money couldn't have been any tighter. Yet, I took the leap of faith and trusted that this had come into my life at this time for a reason. It was more than worth it, as I now experience almost constant peace and contentment in every moment of my life. (Although, my kids can still rattle me at times. Lol!)

Almost two years to the day after I began working with my teacher, she transitioned out of the physical world. Not long after that, her teachings were no longer available to the public. In the midst of my grief, I knew that not only had I lost my teacher and friend, but the world had lost an invaluable resource to rediscover divine truth and navigate the ascension process.

It was at this time that I felt called to make sure that my teacher's legacy lived on and continued to help assist humanity's ascension and, in particular, those struggling with their twin flame journey.

This was when and why I wrote my first book, *Twin Flames Exposed*. In it, I dispel the most common myths which had been created surrounding the twin flame journey, and which so infuriated my dear teacher.

I had no plans to do anything else regarding twin flames or ascension, but my soul (and, I know, my teacher) seemed to have other plans for me.

Another truth:
You do not find your purpose…your purpose finds you.
After my book was published, I began receiving

requests from readers to help guide them along their twin-flame journey. That's when I wrote my downloadable teachings called "The Process."

I thought that would suffice, but, once again, my soul and teacher had other plans.

I was getting inundated with requests to coach people personally along their journeys. At first, I did not want to do this. The resistance I felt to becoming a coach wasn't due to the fact that I didn't care about or empathize with these people. On the contrary, I knew exactly what they were all experiencing (and why).

Resistance is fear, and I was scared shitless to attempt such an endeavor. Who was I to coach or teach people anything? I was still learning myself.

But then, after much internal struggle, I remembered what my teacher's ultimate lesson had always been.

"Trust and believe in yourself."

And so, resonating with that truth (and nothing else), I took a leap of faith and began to offer 1-on-1 coaching. It was scary! Nonetheless, I persevered.

I was truly helping people!

The requests for my coaching services grew. Soon, I wasn't able to keep up with the demand, and I knew I needed to come up with some other way to help more people.

I hired my first of three amazing business coaches to help me. It might sound like an ascension teacher and business coach would have very little similarities, but I was so grateful to my soul for leading me to a business coach who understood the importance of trusting and believing in yourself.

She helped me to remember to do that as I created my very first online/group coaching program helping people experiencing a twin-flame journey overcome their obsessive thoughts and pain and enjoy loving physical relationships with their twin flames if they choose to do so. My program is based on the teachings of my amazing teacher so that I may continue to share and expand her legacy every day.

My program has grown since then and has helped hundreds of people advance along their twin-flame journeys. It's also helped many people who are not currently experiencing a twin-flame journey overcome grief, heartbreak, addiction, depression, anxiety, insecurities, and financial issues – just to name a few of its benefits.

As such, I am now adapting it to resonate with a wider group of people because truth is truth…no matter who you are or what you are currently experiencing.

The key to happiness in every area of life is, of course, you.

How to Get Everything You Truly Desire

Just because you might need guidance resonating with (remembering) yourself on the energetic soul level of love (like I did), doesn't mean that you aren't perfect or that you don't trust and believe in yourself.

I have many coaches who all introduce me to new facets of myself that I learn to trust and believe in.

When someone or something comes in that you resonate with, take that leap of faith and go all in. Jumping without a net is scary, but there is really no better way to show yourself and the Universe that you trust and believe in yourself.

Trusting and believing in yourself – not only in your mind but energetically/on the level of the soul – shifts your energy to one of acceptance, allowing and receiving. This is what is referred to as the state of "pure potentiality."

This opens up space for everything you desire to come right to you.

Your soul and the Universe actually dump it all at your feet! (Of course, if you aren't in a receptive energetic mode, then you'll probably miss it).

Every time I was asked to go all-in on something, it turned out to be a huge game-changer in my life. Immediately after jumping in despite the fear, I was always rewarded in the hugest ways with exactly what I truly desired.

I would never have had the courage to overcome my fear, time and again, if I didn't trust and believe in myself.

And so, that is my secret to success in every area of my life. It's so simple – but not very easy most of the time.

Trusting and believing in yourself is how you love yourself. By accepting all that your soul is orchestrating without judging it as "good" or "bad" is loving yourself and loving whomever and whatever comes into your world, as well.

To clarify, acceptance does not mean that you must engage with everyone or take part in every opportunity or situation that presents itself.

"Acceptance" merely means acknowledging it from a neutral standpoint: "*Okay. This person has shown up in my life offering me a certain opportunity*."

It does not mean that you necessarily jump into every

opportunity or relationship. *"This person is here presenting this opportunity, and that's perfect. But I'm not resonating with this person or opportunity at this time, so I'll pass on it."*

Or, *"This person is here presenting this opportunity, and that's perfect. I'm resonating with this person and opportunity, so I'm going to go for it."*

If/when you go for it – go all-in!

Choosing what you want to do in every moment is trusting and believing in yourself, as well. And trust and believe that there is no "right" or "wrong." No regrets.

Everything truly happens for a reason, and that reason is always to help you grow and expand your consciousness. If you are meant to learn a certain lesson, and you pass up an opportunity to do so, your soul will continue to present you with situations and opportunities to teach you that lesson until you learn it.

You can't get off that easily.

And you can <u>never</u> fool yourself.

You can't fake any of this.

Trust and belief in yourself are authentic and genuine because they happen on the energetic level of the soul, and energy never lies.

I've witnessed some amazing and, one might think, "impossible" things happen on a daily basis throughout my journey and those of my students. My mind is blown constantly (which is understandable since this far surpasses the mind, anyway).

Always believe that something wonderful is about to happen because something wonderful is always happening. Every moment is miraculous and magical because anything is possible.

Anything is possible…as long as you trust and believe in yourself.

"You need not leave your room. Remain sitting at your table and listen. You need not even listen, simply wait. You need not even wait, just learn to become quiet, still and solitary. The world will freely offer itself to you to be unmasked. It has no choice; it will roll in ecstasy at your feet."

~ Franz Kafka

XOXO…

Elle Hari xx

Power Summary

Let's do a quick recap so that you can grasp the key concepts:

1. What are the divine truths that my teacher taught me?

2. What is the state of "pure potentiality"?

3. What must be overcome when you resonate with an opportunity that presents itself to you?

Success Actions

Here are three success actions that you can begin right now to allow things to shift for you and to magnetize what you truly desire into your life:

1. Practice being present and aware of your thoughts. You are not your mind; you are your soul. Become the observer of your thoughts. You can contact us if you need help:

   admin@bewithyourtwinflame.com

2. What parts of yourself and your life are you judging as "good" or "bad"? Tell yourself that they are neither. Everything simply "is," and it's exactly the way it's meant to be in every moment because everything happens for a reason.

3. Be brave. Courage isn't the absence of fear. It's having fear but doing something anyway. When you truly resonate with an opportunity, person, or situation – go all-in!

About the Author

Elle Hari is an ascension and twin-flame alchemist, writer, teacher, and coach. She is the founder and managing partner of Elle Hari Universal, LLC which has, as its sole mission: "assisting humanity's ascension."

Under the Be With Your Twin Flame® division of the company, Elle created of her widely popular and successful "Magnetize Your Twin Flame® Coaching Program;" "The Process™: Do-It-Yourself System," and she wrote the books *Twin Flames Exposed* and *Love Exposed*, both available on Amazon. She is also the creator of *Twin Flame Truth® TV* all episodes of which can be viewed on her Be With Your Twin Flame® *YouTube* channel.

Elle is currently creating an online learning program designed to help people who are not necessarily on a twin-flame journey overcome a myriad of issues ranging from depression, PTSD, and grief, to financial troubles and narcissistic co-dependency utilizing, among other things, the divine truths and energetic work taught to her by her teacher, Liora.

Elle lives at the beach in Florida where, in her free time, she can often be found gazing upon and feeding her soul with the true magnificence of the ocean and the stars.

Business Name: Elle Hari Universal, LLC

Website: www.bewithyourtwinflame.com
Email: admin@bewithyourtwinfalme.com

Facebook: https://www.facebook.com/twinflameteacher/

Instagram: @bewithyourtwinflame

LinkedIn: Elle Hari

Services:
- Magnetize Your Twin Flame® Coaching Program
- "The Process™: Do-It-Yourself System"
- "Twin Flames Exposed"
- "Love Exposed"

Success Is My Destiny

Dr. Hanim Romainoor
Senior Lecturer and Graphics Consultant, Penang, Malaysia

"Ships don't sink because of the water around them; ships sink because of the water that gets in them."

The Dead End

When I was in 18, I felt like a loser, riddled with uncertainties. I was a late reader. I started reading when I was 12 years old. I have dyslexia. I often confuse the letters "B" and "D." I developed the belief that I will fail. Why can't I read? I have worked hard to learn to read. I still fail. How come I keep experiencing failure? And, I did not understand what it means to be a lifelong learner.

I failed my Malay language test. It was in the year 1998. As I collected my certificate "*Sijil Pembelajran Malaysia*" grade slip, I saw my grade list. It was an embarrassing moment. Not a pretty sight for a kid to show their parents. I thought to myself that I had failed my parents because they could not brag about their child's success. I did not understand why I had very bad grades even though I studied very hard, I went to after-school classes, and even had a private tutor for other subjects, especially in my Malay language, physics, biology, chemistry subjects.

But then again, all tests were presented in the Malay language, so, nearly failing the test was expected. It was an embarrassing moment. I felt like the loser of all losers despite getting an A in my English language test. I did not see getting an A in English a privilege. All I could think about was that I could not be a successful person. This was when I developed my bad habit of thinking, "*I am a loser, and I will fail if I don't have a success bar.*"

In my young adult years, though, it was very hard. I set my imaginary bar of success so high that it was very hard to reach, even I myself had trouble reaching it. The bar of success led me to over-comparing myself with others. I would compare my abilities with others who were way ahead of me in their skillset. Often, I felt intimidated, and I would let my ego thoughts weigh me down – telling myself, "*You are a loser!*" Yup, I led myself to overthink that I am not eligible to be honored, even with the commitment I have put in. I also thought that I was never going to be best at what I do. When that overwhelming feeling got inside my head, I would shut down. I ignored my ambitions, hopes, and dreams – including the success bar. I would lay in my bed for hours doing nothing. It was safe. Doing nothing and idling was safe. There, I was safe from becoming a failure.

I did not look back after getting my result. I set a goal that I would reach my success bar and I would get the highest education level. I wanted to continue my studies in a foreign country, and I wanted to become financially free. I wanted to buy my own car and buy my own house before I reached 30 years old. It was 2001. I was listening to Jimmy Eat World singing "The Middle," and part of the lyric stayed in my head:

"Don't write yourself off yet, it's only in your head you feel left out or looked down on, just try your best. Try everything you can..."

Although, I had set my success bar with measurement, I knew I will achieve my goals before I hit 30 years old, and, I knew I had set a goal that I can achieve, even though I failed my Malay language test. It was then that my goal-getter ego was born. My ego would handle my vulnerable feelings; it also will not let me fail. If I did fail, my ego would tell me that I am a loser. My ego became a bad habit and worked hard to make sure that I will not fail a test. My ego saved me from failure but kept me further away from fear. Eventually, I developed a deep fear of failure.

In my story, I'm opening up with you about my journey of commitment and confidence. Sharing with you my *"Yes, I Can!"* Every time when I learn a new skill or a new concept when it seems like there are no more hours left in my schedules to learn, and when I am face to face with too many failures, it seems like quitting is the only solution to move on. I'm sharing with you what the "thing" was that kept me from becoming the real me.

Achieve Just to Fail Yet Again

I did not go back and retake the test. I was convinced it would not take me anywhere, and it would not contribute any benefit to my success bar if I went back or consider to retake my Malay Language test. Having a pass in Malay language test will lead me to work with the government sector (because the government required their staff to be fluent in writing and reading in Malay language) and I believed if I retook the test, I would never pass. So, I continued my life working in the private sector.

Because I had an A in English, I got the opportunity to study in New Zealand. I graduated with high distinction and life is a blessing. Upon coming back to Malaysia, I landed a high-paying job in the private sector. I would job-hop from one private company to another to get as much experience that I could. Three years in the private sector helped me a lot. It sharpened my skills and confidence to work with clients. Also, I got experience as an artist and designer by working with programmers who were audio-video experts in the industry. I was given the opportunity to acquire managerial skills. I was eventually given the position as executive team leader to design instructional, interactive educational CD ROMs.

I continued my job until I came across a chance to continue my Master's and Ph.D. work with a scholarship in Australia. But, in return, I had to work in the government sector. I automatically said, "No," but my mother convinced me to give it a try and submitted the application form. She convinced me that it was 50:50 chance – acceptance or rejection. I was sure I would get rejected due to my language results.

Surprise! I got a letter stating, "*Congratulations! You are invited for an interview.*" So, I went for the interview still thinking they are other candidates who are better than I am, so I won't get it. Weeks passed, and I finally got the call telling me I got the position to continue my Master's and Ph.D. I was shocked! I had mixed feelings of joy and fear. I am still haunted by my failure of my failure in the Malay language, but I had joy that somebody recognized my ability. Fear – what would happen if I had to retake the Malay language test again? And I feared that I would fail that test.

The Call to Adventure

Yes. I got a scholarship to study abroad. I never thought that I would get it. My Malay language failure still haunts me. I felt like an imposter. When meeting my mentor in Australia, I realised that I was good at designing using the computer, and I know when I work hard enough, I will get what I want and I don't need expertise in the Malay language to help me through to my success. I don't need to read or write in the Malay language. My skill and creativity in creating and designing will lead me to my success. I can get what I want to be successful. But, upon meeting my supervisor, my mentor, he said when we first met, *"Hanim, you will experience a lot more failures by the end of your Master's and Ph.D. journey. You will experience failure that will change what you believe about failure itself, and you will experience self-fulfillment and will be at peace with your failure."*

My Master's degree went smoothly. What was the lesson? I didn't get it. The initiation with my supervisor started me on my journey to learn new concepts and ideas. I was at the threshold of my ego. I wanted to look good. I really did not want to fail anymore. I would strategise about how not to fail. I would avoid activities that made me look bad. Then came my Ph.D. degree, in which I experienced a lot of hiccups. I completed my Ph.D. study within four years. I received a lot of critical comments from my external examiner. The comments from the examiner were truthful, and my ego couldn't believe it. I'd build a wall around myself so that I would never fail again.

Here I am, face to face with 10 pages of lists that have comments on my thesis about things I needed to fix. It took me one year to accept the comments. I could not accept the judgment. But I continued anyway, picked up the pieces, and went through my thesis comments slowly, one by one.

I felt failure would kill me, and I wouldn't get my Ph.D., and then I could not work in the government sector due to my weakness in the Malay language. Eventually, I would have to pay back my scholarship. Oh, the trials and failure! I was forced to face my failure. I was really scared.

"*Yes, I Can!*" I began to grow new confidence by sheer force of will. I began to start a daily routine to understand each and every comment presented. Finally, I amended my thesis Ph.D. as requested for each comment. Eventfully, I completed my correction, and I successfully delivered my correction back to my external examiner. I was relieved, and their response was, "*What took you too long? The comments were guidance for you to correct the section that sounded confusing.*" To my surprise, if I had known what the process was all about, I would not have spent so much time thinking about my failure or dare to consider that I would fail at the end of the process.

Breakthrough and Lessons Learned

I discovered my weakness is fear of failure. I also wanted to look good because I didn't want to look like a loser. If I failed, I would not get to my destination which is my success. I developed a belief in my mind that I did not need to pass the test in the Malay language. Of course, my skillset, which enables me to create and design, will push me to reach my success bar. I also have a managerial skillset from my work in the industry. But in all these, I wanted to look at as only good excuses, but what I have now built was an ego that would protect me from failure.

Yes! I passed and graduated with a Ph.D. I am now a Doctor of Philosophy. But, yet again, I faced another failure. As expected, I was required to pass a Malay language test. The fear of failure crept back in. I have a Ph.D., and I still need to take the Malay language test. My ego really hated this situation. But I was then a changed person, and I believed now that this was an opportunity for something, yet another trial I needed to go through. Not once, but twice! I took my Malay language test twice. Once, at the high school level and another at the university level. I controlled my ego and my fear of failure, I studied and practiced the language. Shockingly, I learned to like the Malay language. I realised it is a beautiful language. I finally passed the test and finally was able to let go of my fear of failure.

Now, what is the lesson here? Why didn't I keep on fearing failure? What did I learn from this? What is the growth that I had, and what did I learn from failure? In my act of making amends with myself, I learned that the goal is staying on the path. It is not about looking good or looking bad. I am finally at peace with my Malay language. To my surprise, it teaches me that I don't need to be ignorant of a subject or be arrogant that I do not need to learn it. I should instead accept it and learn to understand the beauty of a new concept or a new idea. I am able to understand how to write well in the Malay language better than before. I can detect spelling and grammar errors in the Malay language faster. I used to find it very difficult to do that. I often quit too early before I learned a new concept.

The gift for me is that I am bilingual. I am an English-speaker and writer, and a fluent Malay writer and speaker. I benefit from both worlds. I learned to be humble with knowledge, because the more I know, the more I don't know. Every hardship I face when learning something new is a new blessing.

If I am in a sinking boat and there is only one life jacket, I want to be the person wearing the life jacket to live a fulfilling life because I have so much to give society and a lot of new and old experiences to share. I have an adventurous story to tell my children. I do not want to die in a sunken ship.

"*Yes, I Can!*" I stopped acting and revealed my failures, weaknesses, and setbacks. I hold myself big. I am not offering a service, but I am willing to serve with the knowledge that I have much to give and much to gain. I am not afraid to learn and face hardships while learning something new. I have built a healthy confidence instead of being arrogant of having only one skillset and not wanting to be open to another skillset that I find hard to learn. The greatness is already inside me. I learn to be real by just being me. I am not ashamed to shine. The world needs my light.

The Wisdom

Tips to be successful:

Perhaps the best you can hope for on your journey – whether you are an artist, designer, a manager, in marriage, or in sports – it is to cultivate your mind and set your heart as being the beginner at every stage along the way in your life journey. To become successful, you need to surrender yourself, which means surrender to understand that there are no experts. There are only learners. You are only in a battle with yourself, not with other people because winning is only the consolation prize. The true meaning of winning is in the process of staying on the path of practice.

"Be you. The real you. Drop the act. Reveal your failures, your weaknesses, your setbacks. Be you, that is what will bring out the greatness which you already have inside of you!"

Dr. Hanim Romainoor

Power Summary

Let's do a quick recap so that you can grasp the key concepts:

1. What failures keeps you from becoming the real you?

2. What experiences are holding you back from moving forward?

3. What is controlling you, and preventing you from being the real you?

Success Actions

Here are four success actions that you can take right now to make things happen in your life:

1. Write down the three main goals that you want to accomplish in the next 90 days.

2. Create a list of professional and personal goals.

3. Write down your goals and tell a friend.

4. Be rigorous in your efforts to achieve your goals in the next 90 days.

Hanim Romainoor

About the Author

Dr. Hanim Romainoor is a Senior Lecturer and currently holds the position as the Head of Department of Graphic Communication at School of The Arts, Universiti Sains Malaysia. She is a researcher and educator. Her research interests are graphics/design research, typography and future technology. In class, she coaches students to understand graphic design elements and principles. She has experience working in the private industry as a multimedia graphic designer. Her designs range from book covers to UI/UX websites. She gained design management skills by attending a course on Capability Maturity Model Integration (CMMI) in 2006 and achieved certification which qualified her to lead the creative team in the production of interactive CD-ROMs. She also loves doing consultant works and supporting people with their design projects.

Business Name: Senior Lecturer and Graphics Consultant. Also, Head of Department of Graphic Communication at School of The Arts, Universiti Sains Malaysia.

Website: https://art.usm.my/graphic/

Email: hanim.romainoor@gmail.com

Facebook: Hanim Romainoor

Instagram: hanimromainoor

LinkedIn: https://www.linkedin.com/in/hanim-romainoor-486599120/

Products/Services: Design Masterclass and Literature Review Masterclass

Ideal Clients: Academics, Researchers, and Designers

The Value I Needed to See

Jairrod A. Burch (Mr. Value)
Expert Value Empowerment Speaker/Author and Value Life Coach Specialist, United States

"We are cheating ourselves if we dream of excellence but settle only for average."

~ Jairrod A. Burch

When Purpose Calls

Have you ever had that feeling that you just couldn't shake?

I mean, no matter how you tried to suppress it, ignore it, or even evade it, you just couldn't seem to let it go! More importantly, <u>it wouldn't let you go!</u>

At night you dream of it. When you're up going throughout your day, you're daydreaming of it! In conversations with friends and family, you find yourself always coming around to mentioning it in some way.

What is it exactly?

"It is the thing that is ultimately your internal GPS system. It's the thing that you gravitate to effortlessly. Yes, even that very thing that seems so far out of reach somehow continues to pull at your heart continuously.

That thing is called your "Purpose."

It's the very reason you were designed and placed here on Earth! At least that's how it is with me.

I didn't always know that I would be who I am today. I didn't always know that I would be in a position to affect, transform, and influence people's lives, but it all started with a call and my decision to either pick it up or to allow that call to go unanswered.

I grew up in a small town with my parents and four older brothers. Life was rough, to say the least! We didn't have much, but we had each other – that was until my oldest brother moved out of the house and my parents divorced.

Life seemed already unbearable before the split. It was in those times that I would have a glimpse of my destiny – just enough to let me know that no matter how bad things were, I knew somehow my story wouldn't end there.

Now, you may be wondering what all of this has to do with you and your path to success!

I'm here to let you know that success is not defined by material luxury. No. That's only a momentary preference. I'm not talking about what you acquire to impress others. I'm talking about understanding the value of discovering your Purpose to impact the world around you.

You see earlier, I spoke about how "it" is always calling out to you in some way, shape, or form. "It," being the things that you were equipped with and designed to do that would help transform the lives of others around you.

Aka…your <u>Purpose</u>!

The reason why it was so important to realize that something greater was waiting for me was, so I did not give up where I messed up. Whether it was the abuse I suffered, coming from a broken home, struggling not having enough, battling depression, fighting off thoughts of suicide, going through a divorce as I got older, and much, much more.

I need you to understand that despite what you have been through and are facing now, everything you've endured serves as a victory that you can use from your personal experiences, good or bad, to share with others to allow them to see proof that life can throw the worst at you.

It's how you decide to <u>respond</u> to these challenges that is going to determine your setbacks or comebacks.

Those glimpses of greatness and Purpose are so necessary in your life. In fact, they may even seem like a real nuisance at times because they come in moments when you could need them the most, times when you're down and completely out – those times when you're at your rock bottom. The last thing you want to see in your visions are glimpses of you graduating from college, or visions of you going back to school at an older age.

Or visions of you starting your own business. Dreams of becoming an owner of multiple properties. Clips of seeing yourself getting married…again, and it being the right relationship this time.

It's like, *"Why show me visions of <u>greater</u> when all I can see around me is the reality of <u>worse</u>?"*

Please, please, please…understand the Purpose is always <u>bigger</u> than just that one moment.

When you see these visions, and you see these dreams, when you stop believing that they are just silly and start believing that even if they seem so far out of reach, you can achieve them!

The moment you become crazy enough to believe that you can achieve what you're seeing is when you have answered the call and made the first step into one of the greatest moments in your life.

What Do I Do After I Say Yes?

So, what do you do after you have made the leap from fear to further in stepping out into your destiny? Each situation and answer for each individual will be different.

For me, I always knew that I had a gift to speak, but I didn't know to the full extent of what it would look like. I grew up in church and was in a family full of ministers, so quite naturally, I thought it would just be all about ministry. Little did I know that the plan for my life was much larger than the eyes I was seeing them through.

So, fast forward to the future!

In 2015, I had already heard the call and my Purpose had already been getting on my nerves and kicking my butt to step out already, so I started my business:

Value on Purpose with Jairrod A. Burch, LLC

This was my speaking, coaching and consulting company. I had already been traveling and speaking since I was 15 years old, so speaking was not a problem. However, now because of the things I had been through and experienced in my life, I had not only something to say but now I had a diverse group of individuals to speak my message to.

I was speaking and sharing my message of "understanding your value" and "knowing your Purpose" to large radio platforms, sports organizations, high schools, and hosting podcast shows that reached over seven different nations, coaching and consulting business professionals, entrepreneurs, and more.

What am I saying all of this to you?

I am trying to get you to understand that you have a Purpose for a Purpose. The gifts and talents that you possess are in you so that you can inspire and impact those around you.

Your story! Yes, your story!

The good, bad, and the ugly parts are the exact ingredients needed to help so many others in their struggles in life.

But first, it starts with:

- Know that you have a greater Purpose in your life.

- Find those who can help you identify that Purpose in your life.

- Make the decision to step out of fear and step into faith concerning your destiny.

- After you make the decision to step out into whatever your specific Purpose is, make a commitment to stay with it.

- Develop and sharpen your skills so that you can expand your influence.

- Surround yourself with a support system, not a support group. (Big difference...)

These are the things that you will need to understand after you answer the call because saying "Yes!" is an <u>action</u> word!

That's what makes Purpose so powerful.

It is so powerful it has helped me being able to come from being poor, from abuse, from brokenness, pain, loss, divorce, failure after failure and defeat, to still being able to decide not to give up in my earlier chapters of despair. Purpose has helped me in becoming an influencer, speaker, author, advocate, life coach, and business owner.

And all this was not because I was special, nor was it because I had any special hook-ups to get me to where I am today. I was just blessed to be able to understand that there was a value that I needed to see within me. This was the value that said, "*You are not what you are going through.*

You're more than your mistakes, and even you can help others to discover their worth no matter what they face in life."

As my company's motto says, *"I'm bringing value back into the lives of many, one experience at a time."*

I am now able to help individuals who can only look at themselves to being able to actually see themselves!

Let me help you with the value you need to see within you.

Jairrod A. Burch

A Recap of How You Can Activate these Power Principles:

- Know that you have a Purpose in this life.

- You need others to help you find what that is.

- Understand that your value is your story in your life, no matter how bad things are.

- Know that you have influence in your story.

Four Keys to Action Towards Discovering the Value You Need to See Within <u>You</u>

- Make a decision TODAY to believe in YOURSELF!

- Step out and step up in the dreams that you have.

- Find a coach that can help push you towards that dream.

- Don't just discover your value and Purpose, but commit to following it all the way through.

"Keep it simple to set yourself up for your success."
~ Jairrod A. Burch

About the Author

Jairrod A. Burch, (Mr. Value) has been speaking since the age of 15 years old.

It was then as a youth that it was instilled into his heart that there was a great purpose for his life. Experiencing many trials and challenges, Jairrod was being developed and sharpened to soon be able to add value to the world around him, and abroad.

In 2015 that's when Value on Purpose was born! It came after 25 years of training and traveling the country, inspiring others. It was now time to expand and exert his influence onto the lives of many who needed to understand their worth.

Now, as an Expert Value Empowerment Speaker, Author, Podcast Host, CEO, and Value Life Coach Specialist, it is not only his passion, but his responsibility to push, pull, and propel individuals into their greatness by showing them how to operate in their fullest valued potential.

Business Name: Value on Purpose with Jairrod A. Burch, LLC

Website: www.valueonPurpose.com

Email: Contact@ispeakvalue.com

Facebook: Jairrod A. Burch

Instagram: Jairrodaspeaks

LinkedIn: Jairrod A. Burch

Products/Services: Keynote Speaker/ Consulting/Value Life Coach Specialist & Author

Ideal Clients: Universities, Sports Organizations, High Schools & Corporations.

The Power of Mindfulness

Julie Britton
Life and Business Coach, Wales

"Practicing acceptance and non-judgment sets us free and liberates us."

~ Julie Britton

The Unthinkable

Losing everything gave me everything! When I was 38 years old, my Mum was diagnosed with Motor Neuron Disease. The ripples of consequences that flowed from a critically ill and widowed mother lead to an enormous series of life-changing events that felt like a shattering earthquake. Little did I know how losing a loved one could affect us on so many levels – mentally, emotionally, physically, and spiritually. The pain of grief is overwhelming and inescapable.

Accepting the things that we cannot change has been the most powerful yet painful and liberating lesson of my life. Would you have guessed it was possible to manifest and double your turnover during an emotional crisis?

The Conflict

I'm not loveable, I'm wrong, I'm bad, I'm alone, I'm separate, I'm not seen, I'm not heard, I'm not included, I worry what-if, I am powerless.

I remember sitting at the dinner table, six years old, and enjoying a small, family gathering. Getting a hard slap across the head for saying something wrong was a regular thing. Through many personal-development courses and coaching sessions, I have now forgiven my parents and was able to restore love, friendship and reconcile our past. After many years of physical and emotional abuse as a child, I have now let go of all the judgment which has provided a new kind of relatedness with my mother. I encouraged my mother to participate in personal development also so that we could complete our past so that the latter years of our relationship was transformed into the best friendship.

The Breakthrough and Lessons Learned

I threw myself into my work of making a difference and success after success followed. The many successes I achieved through my business could not mask the pain when my office door shut. The one thing that helped it pass was practicing breathing-and-sitting techniques that I had learned and implemented from my Mindfulness teachings. The practice gave me access to freedom, saying hello to the pain and breathing into the loss, like welcoming a dear old friend. Giving myself space and time in a highly scheduled diary of clients was making a difference.

This quiet time helped me evaluate who my true friends were and to let go of the ones that were more toxic than nurturing while embracing who I am as a woman and following through my trusted answers with inspired actions.

Who would have believed what it would take to

balance? It took integrating my whole self by balancing my mind, my body and soul, consciously waking up to my shadow-self, and dynamically living my life by accepting its realities.

The Ordinary World

Educated through the medium of the Welsh language, I grew up in a Welsh valley town with high unemployment and working-class parents with strong work ethics who focussed on values and ideals of discipline, hard work, and providing overbearing parental control. The idea of success was cultivated in the family home by teaching the values of leading and following, and conforming to the rigid rules. All of these were designed to form good habits for staying motivated so as to be successful in one's career. My ordinary world consisted of often feeling a burning rage when dragged into compliance and pushed into passivity against my will. All of this was covered with a mask of smiles and laughter to protect the family identity.

The Drama

Because of the inner hunger and drive to achieve my greatest potential and find my true vocation in life while having my parents be proud of me, I had real problems with feelings of being bad and wrong at the core. I had real difficulties with rebellious behaviour and accepting my mother. I felt a real need to follow the crowd and experience the problems that arose in risk-taking behaviours during adolescence and engaged in reckless, risky, and thrill-seeking behaviours such as smoking, alcohol, sex, drugs, and dating violence.

This style of parenting and upbringing affected me in not being able to recognise and protect my own wise needs, values, and desires in the area of relationships.

The Turning Point

My coaching business and career success was on the upswing. I was working at full capacity with my business thriving financially. The coaching is really making a difference to the quality of my business and to the many lives and businesses of others after forgiving my parents and the past journey so far. Little did I know that another crisis was on its way when everything came to a head after the loss of my mother. I had a partner with ADHD, a mental illness that affects one's mood, thinking, and the ability to recognise other people's needs and desires. We were unaware, frustrated, and confused. It was undiagnosed, and we were living with major symptoms that interfered with daily functioning in everyday life. This was all combined with having no idea why my levels of energy were so low and deeply fatigued and why I was irritable and having difficulty concentrating from the onset of the menopause, which was also undiagnosed. Underneath all the daily mayhem sat a deep well of sadness, sorrow, and loneliness which prevailed since losing my mum. It bored right into me rather than skating over my skin. It travelled deep into every cell, reaching down to the ground, leaving me feeling like I was, drowning in my own suppression of emotion.

This continued until one day while taking a walk, everything changed. I practiced gratitude. I felt I was so blessed. I love where I lived. The sky was clear blue. It gave me clarity. The air was calm. I felt a freedom. I felt comforted with the sun kissing me upon my face. The green rolling hills brought comfort and wrapped around me like a patchwork quilt. Alone, finally, and consoled by the freedom evoked from the miles of hills, a wailing sound came from up out of my mouth from deep within my belly. The tears rolled out. My frustration and burden were released. I felt like an erupting volcano! With every roar came the release of pressure, a flow of insights and answers, the rush of confirmation, and the mixed feelings of comfort and release now knowing the cause of our symptoms. I realised I could take control of these feelings and symptoms.

I rushed home to research ADHD, menopause, and grief.

The Call to Action

I heard my friend, another life and business coach, explain the difference between coaching and Mindfulness. Coaching is a tool to empower people to move them out of their current situation, develop new ways of speaking, thinking, behaviours, and inspired action that empower.

Mindfulness is the practice of being with the feelings, being with the breath, being with the inner thoughts and feelings, while being on purpose, with non-judgment, and accepting those feelings of abandonment and separation (in my case), which were leading to unhealthy habits of sabotage. Comfort-eating and drinking alcohol were small moments of pleasure and happiness all adding to the expansive growing wholeness of pain leading ultimately to depression.

After some regular Mindfulness practice, I started to see a way to deal with and respond to the challenges of feelings. As simple as it sounded, experiencing the breath and accepting the discomfort gave me sufficient distance to observe my emotions and make choices that were wise and supportive of my needs.

One of the things I am really good at is being strong,

being empowered, taking new inspired action towards achieving hard outcomes and goals. I had a successful business, regular clients, awareness of who my tribe is to market to, a powerful relationship with money, a beautiful home, and a snazzy car. All these things came effortlessly. It was the way I was brought up – look good and be successful and independent in your own right.

I noticed an increase in energy, a feeling of lightness, and I had control back in my grasp. This journey of Mindfulness is now supporting me to accept the things I cannot change and let go of the pressures I put on myself, while understanding the deeper reality of how habits can further impact my minds health and physical well-being. I soon saw a new product emerging for my business and for the many clients who suffered from hiding their pain behind a mask success, money, and achievement. My interest focused on the new possibilities available for dealing with the chronic trauma in lives associated with death, loss, depression, anxiety, fatigue, post-traumatic stress disorder, burnout, and driven states of workaholic type of behaviours, most of which led to the effort to be comforted by food and drink addictions.

I further adapted and designed current and new courses that included Mindfulness as part of the coaching and training services I provide.

The Downfall

Even though Mindfulness was the new buzzword, my *Facebook* community were responding well. Some of the businesses I worked with were more sceptical given the fast-moving markets they were in. I quickly saw an opportunity to educate those people.

There was a widespread lack of awareness that people carried around knowing what Mindfulness is and the incredible value that could be harnessed through Mindfulness.

I saw the value promoting the power of quieting victim behaviour and self-degrading speaking, and instead, exploring how to take responsibility for oneself by focusing on the positives with gratitude. The practise, itself, creates new brain neurons to wire and fire creating new patterns and letting go of others. It was time for me to join forces with other experts as education on this topic in general was very sketchy. I was inspired to revolutionise the market, so I travelled as far as India through to Austria in search of the true underpinnings of Mindfulness, and as part of my journey, I found the Ayurveda philosophy of life. I have incorporated its teachings into my own Mindfulness philosophies.

The Key Ingredients

I shared my story in front of the right people who were willing to listen. Local friends and clients requested a Mindfulness Clinic to practice these tools. These included clients and friends who were dealing with loss, critical disease, and health matters, married people living with partners with mental health issues, and people experiencing stress and burnout from their working roles.

I designed my own unique class that combined the power of coaching and Mindfulness together. Both parts developed the muscles required to reach fulfilling outcomes in life while developing greater resilience, patience, and peace for dealing with all types of challenges when they arise.

I continued to study the power of the mind and how neuroplasticity can repair the mind, body, and soul.

The Growth

During my training in Mindfulness, I was seen as a change-leader in this unique field and was asked to design a course for young, talented artists to not only embrace the pressures that arise through the "volatile and competitive" nature of the music industry but also to bring the kind of critical thinking that is required to successfully do the balancing and prioritising of the various roles within any business success to thrive.

Since this course, which has been running for four years now, I have now adapted all of my coaching courses, leadership training programs, and Mindfulness workshops and retreats to now include Mindfulness at the core of our work.

The core mantra of my work for any life or business issue that arises for oneself or another includes the four Mindset practises of Observe, Acknowledge, Accept, and Choose a new inspired action for life balance and wisdom about whatever they're dealing with

Another key is that by acknowledging all feelings and thoughts that arise, they provide an inner compass and guidance for our needs and wants which act as stability for us to build our life's goals upon.

I wanted to revolutionise the way we see mental health and depression for leaders and entrepreneurs as a way of us following our own inner guide to live a fulfilling life.

Clients are saying they feel more in control communicating their needs, taking the time to practice Mindfulness distinctions. Customers are saying I enjoy resetting the button for life. I then re-designed my coaching programs with Mindfulness at the core.

Selflove Program – Many clients are now able to articulate the way they feel and practice good, radical, self-care by forgiving themselves and setting boundaries.

Loving the Inner Child – Clients share how they have moved beyond the inner script of how life should be and created new beliefs by letting go of unconscious patterns.

Keeping the Love in Relationships Alive – Letting go of castration and objectification.

Authentic Mindful Leadership – Creating mindful change-leaders revolutionises its industry for profit and well-being.

Gratitude for Prosperity – Having a new value around the relationship to money.

Mindful Structures – Success/Health/Wealth/Well-Being – How to achieve everything in balance.

The Reward

My reward is being able to run a successful business in line with balancing my spiritual, physical, mental, and emotional needs. Another reward is giving back to the youth community encouraging them to be successful while be grounded within a Mindfulness practice and balance for wellness.

I am able to work with young rugby talent in the Ospreys and the Welsh Rugby Union creating the future of Welsh rugby teams and youthful, talented musicians to be able to reach their greatest potential and contribute to our future.

I created a two-year Change Leadership Program for 20 junior managers and salesmen in the fresh produce industry. All the junior salesmen created projects (One project call 'Bann the Blade'- designed to put a stop to gossip, judging, criticism and invalidation of work, raising effective communication, constructive feedback and acknowledgment of work done well with appreciation all of which increased profits by 5% in 1 year) themselves that made a lasting, mindful difference in the way their teams worked efficiently, profitably, and with Mindfulness by speaking from their core values leaving all men validated and respected.

I also own my own house, and it is nearly fully paid for.

A core hub of local community people in my town, Talgarth in Powys, are committed to the power and practice of Mindfulness, and we are represented as Mindfulness leaders in our community.

I am part of a local self-created walking group of 12 amazing women who listen, support, and empower each other.

I love making a holistic difference in the way people choose to live their life successfully with well-being at the core.

I have come down three dress sizes, quite eating dairy, wheat, gluten, reduced my alcohol consumption by two-thirds. I walk or run every week, 10 to 20 miles a month, and eat vegan five days a week.

The Brightness of the Future

My future is to continue to share the power of Mindfulness and leadership combined through the medium of coaching/training programs, creating a new world of performance and well-being so that people enjoy coming to work.

The Wisdom

My wisdom consists of knowing what I now know about the subversion being driven by success, the grief from loss, the changes that occur for women during the menopause, and the stress experienced through living with someone with ADHD.

It also includes making time for habits for health and wellbeing, and meeting our emotions and thoughts observed with non-judgment, the key to acceptance which sets us free and gives us choice.

- Practice daily eyes-open and eyes-shut Mindfulness.

- Avoiding discomfort are dead people's goals.

- Discomfort gives us meaning and resilience.

- It's only a struggle if you resist it and avoid it.

- Remember, you have choice.

- Let go things which are not your responsibility.

"Learn to listen to yourself and take a risk to action your own advice"
~ Julie Britton

Love,

Julie Britton

Three Questions for Reflection

1. How can you best deal with uncomfortable feelings?

2. What are your uncomfortable feelings telling you?

3. What shouldn't you do when you are dealing with uncomfortable emotions?

Mindful Actions

What three actions can you take to help you when you feel overwhelming emotion?

1. Sit and bring your awareness to your breath.

2. Experience your in-breath at its fullness, and out-breath of emptiness.

3. Notice the thoughts that arise, label them, and return awareness back to the breath.

About the Author

Julie Britton is an inspirational life and business coach that revolutionises entrepreneurs, business services and team's performance. Bespoke training and coaching workshops are personally designed according to their needs and delivered to groups and individuals to achieve greater profit, efficiency, and performance with well-being at the core. Transformational leadership programs are developed for senior, junior managers, junior salesmen, rugby athletes, talented musicians, and directors and executives who are dealing with an inner conflict or a performance-related matter that is impacting their business outcomes and aspire to be at their greatest potential.

Business Name: Commit2Action

Website: www.commit2action.co.uk

New website being developed: www.juliebritton.co.uk

Email: Julie.britton@commit2action.co.uk

Facebook: Commit2Action

LinkedIn: Mindfullness/Retreats

Products and Services:
- Training managers and leaders to be a mindful, authentic, and powerful leadership producing team results.
- 121 Coaching for Team: Management, leadership, entrepreneurship, and career development
- Training workshops who want to re-create corporate vision, mission and values, while redefining roles and smart objectives that fit in line with the mission.
- Creating the artist's self-expression of music, breaking through fear and self-loathing, and structuring their success.
- Emotional Intelligence Business System for recognising strengths and weaknesses of business intelligences.
- Non-Violent Communication
- Mindfulness Level 1 & 2 Workshops: Understanding how the brain works and Mindfulness practice for greater resilience.
- Life Coaching for a renewed self-love, self-esteem, and healing of the inner child.
- Couples Coaching for keeping the love in relationships.
- Tools for depression, anxiety, trauma, and grief.

- **Ideal Clients:**

Fast-moving goods industry such as:
- Welsh Rugby Union
- Ospreys Welsh Rugby Management Team
- Total Produce Fresh Produce
- Worldwide Fruit
- S.H. Pratt & CO (Banasa), Ltd
- MMUK Fruit Wholesaler
- Flourish Cymru
- Fort Project Talented musician artists
- Bakers food allied union
- Lafarge Roofing, LTD
- Continental Teves – Car Accessory Manufacturers
- Griffiths Road Construction, Ltd
- Sumtomo Electrical Wiring Looms
- Cwm Garw Welsh Primary School
- Front Row Police Officers in Wales and UK
- The Wallich Charitable & Voluntary Organisation
- British Airways
- Harrods

Dream Team

Lyna Noh
Business Coach, Malaysia

"To make a difference, you must ignite your determination and reinforce it by building your professional ally network."
~ Lyna Noh

The Unthinkable

"You won't make it. I can guarantee this. I knew it because I did it before, and I failed. So will you."

These were my father's "words of encouragement" when I told him about my intention of starting a networking-based business.

My family is a typical family that believed in order to be successful in life, one needs a great career, and it always has to be a government servant. The government provides job security, so you don't have to worry about losing a job or something.

Starting a business? That was out of our way. Furthermore, I already secured a job as an engineer in a number-one, multinational oil and gas company. Why would I need a business?

The Conflict

I am an avid reader, and that has exposed me to many things including the topic of finances, especially financial freedom. From my reading, I learned I wouldn't get financial freedom by having a job. My engineering career won't provide that freedom unless I climb the corporate ladder and become a senior manager, which was not in my plan. I need to start a business so that I could create a higher, or maybe multiple, streams of income.

However, I had no idea where I should start. My family was not involved in business, neither were my friends. To them, either business was too simple or too hard.

To make it worse, they called me "ungrateful" for still pursuing a business while having a decent job.

The Breakthrough and Lessons Learned

I built my own support system by creating a new space in myself for a new circle of friends. They were entrepreneurs and businesswomen from all over Malaysia. I was shy, so I approached them with care. To my surprise, they were very humble and willing to openly share many things with me. And the most important thing was changing my mindset from an employee-thinking style to an entrepreneur-thinking style.

Mindset is everything if you want to start a business. It changed the way I see the world and how I see people. This circle finally became my friends. And guess what? These new friends not only support what I was about to start but also appreciate what I already did!

It was priceless...

The Ordinary World

I grew up in a small village in Kota Bharu in the beautiful state of Kelantan in Malaysia. Since I was a little girl, I was told to study hard and get a job. What made me different from my childhood friends was I knew how to read since before I went to kindergarten. I read a lot beginning at a very young age. According to my parents and my uncles, I read almost everything including the old newspapers we used to wrap food!

I studied really hard, got good grades, and entered a famous university in my country which enabled me to get a job as an engineer. It made my parents so proud but without they're knowing it, a job as an engineer wouldn't make their daughter became financially free as I always dreamed of.

The Drama

I thought the business world was a nice and wonderful world. I dreamed it was like a wonderland where I could swim in a river of money. Little did I know that nearly everything about business is hurtful.

It hurt to be rejected. I was hurt when somebody says *"No."* It was hurt when you don't hit your target. It hurt to be betrayed. I didn't realize that those things were able to drag you down to the bottom.

It was enough to give me sleepless nights. The heartache was unbearable.

The Turning Point

One night, I sat down alone and thought, *"Is this all there is?"*

I got out my smartphone and opened the web browser. I didn't know what I search for, but for sure, I was looking for an answer. After some searching, I came across a story of a lady entrepreneur, her ups and downs, and up again. It reminded me of the first business autobiography book I read some time ago, Sam Walton's *Made in America*. I eventually realized that I already knew what to expect.

Yes!

The Call to Action

I believed that in business, to be successful fast, we needed to be street smart and learn as we work.

Furthermore, I needed to be fast, because I don't have time to waste. I was an engineer, a wife, and a mother. I couldn't afford to waste one more second of my days.

I went back to my business circle, not only as a "circle," but I formed a team with them – a team of entrepreneurs with various experiences in different fields. This team would not only help me but would also other newcomers in this industry.

From that point, I built my own team – a business team that was not only friends in business but friends in life.

The Downfall

It wasn't easy to form a team and more difficult to lead a team of people with a wide range of experience. I came from an engineering background, and it was very simple back then. Everybody knew each others' role, and the team leader's job was to brief and to get updates.

But it was different for the networking business. The majority of the team members don't know what they want and what to do.

The challenge started when you wanted to bring people into the team. Either nobody turned up, or you had many people in, but none of them were the right ones. I faced both of these challenges. Nobody wanted to be on my team, and if there was somebody, she or he was not my "Dream Team" member.

The Key Ingredient

One thing people always talk about business and marketing is branding. Branding is a simple thing but intentionally made complicated by some branding gurus. It is just as simple as, *"How do you see yourself in order to make people trust you?"* Some of us just have little confidence in ourselves, like me in the very beginning.

I used to think that I wasn't enough. I didn't have enough knowledge, not enough experience, and I was not beautiful enough – but these weren't my problem. I was more than enough.

It is because I have a support team that is always with me. I have a hideout place where I can always express my fears and doubts and they are received with no prejudice.

So, I started to "brand" myself. People started to know me, not only by name but by what I was doing and contributing.

The Growth

I saw myself climbing the ladder of success, rung by rung, even though working my full-time job as an engineer. To make sure everything ran smoothly, I created a system that allowed my business to run by itself so it wouldn't interfere with my engineering career.

I wrote several e-books to increase my exposure to the new market and prospects. From there, I grew my business and my team and started to get the right people coming in.

I contributed back to my fellow entrepreneurs who were my support team, by providing them support and free training.

The Reward

I was rewarded as the top recruiters, top income earners, top leaders, kept joining my team every year. My team kept on growing and they plugged into the system. They also get rewarded, grow their own teams, and grow their income.

My business income increased and increased until I was able to tender my resignation from my engineering job. After leaving the corporate world, I had more time for my family, I got to travel to 20 or 30 countries in a year, participate in volunteering activities, and much, much more.

The Brightness of the Future

In this uncertain world, I am certain that I can help many people who want to be an entrepreneur and build their own business by providing support, especially team support.

Nowadays that the economy is unstable, many people lose their jobs, and even if they still have one, sometimes do not enough to fund their dreams. To keep their dreams alive, they need to start a business, and I am here to help them to build a business of their own with low risk and low capital.

The Wisdom

My Seven Secrets to Success:
1. Find a mentor.
2. Work in a team.
3. Learn as you grow.
4. Take charge and be responsible.
5. Plan ahead.
6. Build your own support system.
7. Don't ever give up.

Quote

"Alone, we can achieve a lot. Together, we are unstoppable."

Luv,

Power Summary

A Quick Recap:

1. Do you know that even if your family never has done any business, you still can be successful in business?

2. How would you get support when your loved ones have doubts about your dream?

3. How should you plan so that the team you create becomes a supportive team?

Success Actions

1. Equip yourself with knowledge.

2. Build a support system that can guide and support you.

3. Build your own team so that you can apply what you've learned.

About the Author

Lyna Noh is a brand new, bestselling author of business self-help books. She is an experienced network marketer, blogger, and a wonderful friend. She loves to travel with her family and has been to more than 70 countries. Lyna makes her home in Kuala Lumpur as a place to store all her favorite books and traveling gear, and as a home for her four beautiful children.

Lyna Noh

Business Name: iReach Sdn Bhd

Website: http://ireach.my

Email: lyna@ireach.my

Facebook: web.facebook.com/LynaNoh and web.facebook.com/ireach.my

Instagram: @lynanoh

Products and Services: Business support, Mentoring

Ideal Clients: People who want to build their own business at home.

The High Ticket Formula

Maeve Ferguson
Coach, Northern Ireland

"I could, so I did."
~ Maeve Ferguson

My life was perfect. My career was flying. I loved my job. Managing a team of 50 people was amazing. My other half and I had just bought our little horse farm in Northern Ireland. Life was headed exactly where we wanted it to go. I was 32 years old and had the world at my feet.

It is easy when I look back now, to see signs and patterns of behaviour like overworking, overachieving and pushing to the limit every day. The scariest thing is that I didn't see it coming. Everything came crashing down. I was swimming with my friend, and I didn't feel well. I had a virus.

Initially, I kept pushing myself, doing conference calls from my bed against my boss's persistent requests to stop. A few months later, when I thought I was recovering, I was out for a walk and "the plug came out." I didn't know how I was going to take one more stride, never mind walk home. I spent weeks in bed and weeks on the sofa. I got worse and worse. I couldn't stand for the time it took to have a shower.

I had to buy an electric wheelchair to get around the inside of the house. It was a soul-destroying time.

By year three, the realisation dawned that maybe this was it, that I would never be my old self again. It couldn't be; this was not what our life was supposed to look like. We had so many plans and hopes for all of the things we were going to do. I reached the bottom where things had gotten so bad, there were times that I didn't have the strength to brush my hair. My family, my other half's Mum and Dad, and our friends helped so much, but it was grim.

I tried every "treatment" under the sun, spending thousands of pounds trying to get well. But it just wouldn't go away.

Four years later, when stronger, I re-joined the workplace. A combination of time, mainstream and alternative treatments, things began to take a slow turn for the better. I was able to get out of the wheelchair. I was able to make a cup of tea. I was able to walk a lap around the house. Things seemed possible again, and we started making plans. I was getting another chance.

I begged my doctor to let me get back to work. Eventually, she conceded, but reality hit, and I painfully realised that I wasn't as far on the recovery path as I thought. So, after eight months of trying hard, I left. It was the bravest thing I have ever done. Leaving carried high risk but staying was the riskiest thing to do.

I retrained as a coach and set up a new online business. I now help women create their signature, online service business so that they can live life on their own terms. I absolutely love coaching women and watching them achieve their dreams.

Head over to my website:

www.maeveferguson.com

…to find out more about my program, The High Ticket Formula.

I have learned so much along the way, and these are some of my biggest secrets that will help you on your journey:

1. **Invest in Yourself**
   Get the right results-based Coach – this is critical. So many people struggle and try to go it alone thinking they know better, or worse yet, thinking that they will go and earn some money and <u>then</u> invest in someone who can get them results. Many months, or even years later, they are still struggling. To create a world-class service, you must invest in world-class leaders in their field, and you learn from them. Yes, I spent thousands on excellent programs and mentors, but it was worth it. I learned everything about their craft from their years in the trenches. If you try to figure it out alone, you will still be here in five years trying to sell your products or services for a mediocre fee. It's as simple as that. Identify and face your weak spots. Do your research. Invest in a skilled person that can give you what you need.

2. **Listen to Feedback**
   There is no failure, only feedback. I see so many who are setting up their own businesses, and they get a few "Nos," so naturally, they feel disappointed. They stop, reflect that business is hard, and then they quit. It is so important to remember that any "No" from the market is simply feedback. From that, listen, learn and iterate. It is

absolutely key to listen to your market and then give them exactly what they want.

3. **Believe in Yourself**

   Believe in your ability to figure it out. I love this one! Did I know everything there was to know before I started? Of course not! I hadn't used *Facebook* for years. I didn't even know what digital marketing was. I was horrible at tech – ask Philip, my right-hand man, at my old job! The only business I knew was the corporate world. I thought you had to wear a suit and be formal at all times. Nothing could be further from the truth. So, what do you do when you think you don't know enough? You believe in your ability to figure it out. There is nothing in this world that can't be learned. Any other view is a self-limiting belief, in my opinion.

4. **Sell what People Want**

   Sell before you create – this is key. It also frustrates me that so many out there spend months in their own head, dreaming and planning. They come up with an idea in the shower. Then they spend another few months building it before bringing it to the market and trying to sell it. Then, crickets. Zero. Nothing. Dreams destroyed. Always, (within your ethical boundaries) sell what the market wants, not what you want to sell. Find out what they want before you dream up an idea. Do deep, ninja-level market research so that you understand your market's pulse, your niche vertical, their every thought, everything. Then pre-sell. Then build.

5. **Niche Down Tight**

   Niche down. This one is so critical. I see people trying to be all things to all people and ending up with a "low ticket" offer, chasing after work for little reward. As the saying goes, "She who chases many rabbits catches none. She who chases one, wins." Even go as far as choosing one vertical within a niche, so that you become the go-to expert in that niche, globally.

6. **Be Consistent**

   Consistency matters. This is another weakness that I notice. Many women that I work with often start their business and do things sporadically, maybe because they are juggling so many other demands. Or conversely, they go crazy at it, don't get results within a month, and then stop. Then they wonder why they are not earning six or seven figures. Consistency matters. You cannot show up inconsistently and expect your business to grow. It isn't a business if you do; it's a hobby. Even when you are having a rough day or week, do your mandatory tasks every single day.

7. **Surround Yourself with the Right People**

   I love this one! People with limiting beliefs and a scarcity mindset do not belong in your life if you are going to become a success. People that suck the life out of you, people who drain you, people who pressurise you into being less – stay away from them. Anyone who isn't your greatest cheerleader should not be in your life. Simple. Surround yourself with winners and you too shall win.

8. **Get Results**

   Results are all that matter for your clients. I think this one is so massive, especially in the online world. There are so many awful, information-based products out there that simply don't get results. It's no wonder their owners are trying to flog them for $97. People don't buy information; they buy results. So, make sure what you do actually gets results. Then your clients become your greatest cheerleaders and you have created a flywheel business. Success and growth become a self-fulfilling prophecy.

9. **Focus on your Clients**
   Clients care about themselves, not you. This is a bit of an "Ah-ha!" moment when you start out. You think everyone cares, and everyone will be judging you and caring about what you wear, what you say, your accent, your location, what you post on *Facebook*, etc. Nothing could be further from the truth. People care about themselves. The only thing that matters to your clients is them. So, stop being obsessed about what everyone will think of you. No one cares.

10. **Get Uncomfortable**
    If you are comfortable, you are not growing. If every day is easy and you are not being stretched, you are stagnant. I remember the first time I posted on social media for my business. I cringed. A little bit of me died. It took me months to be brave enough to put myself out there. But once I did, I laughed at myself and wondered why I had been so worried about it. Things exploded when I got out of my comfort zone. You can't be successful and hide. Simple as that. So, get out of your own head and get uncomfortable.

11. **Create an Automated, Scalable Business**
    The more success your customers have, the more customers you get, which is amazing. But if you are doing one-to-one, you will max out very quickly. You cannot scale as there is physically only one of you and even if you decide to work 20 hours a day, you will still have a maximum client base that you can manage. This means your revenue is going to have a cap. If you don't automate and build a service that can be scaled with ease, i.e., if it relies heavily on you, then you cannot

scale your business. You need to build a service that you can build once and sell over and over. Of course, you will iterate and improve this "one build," but you can sell the same service to an unlimited number of people. Not just the ten that you can cope with in person.

12. Create a High Ticket Ladder

When your clients get amazing results, they want to continue to work with you at a higher price point. So, I always advise my clients that the same applies to them. They should have their base offer, e.g. 2K. Then, from this client base, some will rise to the top and will be smashing it. So, create a VIP offer at a much higher price point for these clients. They will be more than willing to pay, as they know the results they can get from working with you. Then, from that base, create an even higher ticket offer for your mastermind or annual 121 support. And so, it continues. Every single day add clients to your base program, and from these, clients will rise and join you on your highest ticket services.

13. Be Clear About Why You Are Running Your Business

Always scale your business with your "Why" in mind. This is a personal one for me. Each and every one of us has our own "Why." Mine isn't yours, and yours isn't mine. So. what is your "Why?" Why do you want it so badly? Why do you want to do it?

My life has been pretty great to be honest, and I know how fortunate I am. We live in Northern Ireland, close to family and friends, and we own a small horse farm. All that is pretty wonderful, in my opinion. I have an amazing husband who really does believe in me, and we are expecting our first baby, so we are beyond excited. Our dog, Cooper, is a red setter and quite possibly the most amazing dog ever born! I came from a brilliant family of six kids, our Mum and Dad worked hard, and we were brought up with a quiet but strong belief in ourselves. We were loved and supported, and not reaching for the sky was not an option. That grounding and base helped me be successful. If you didn't have it, that's ok; create your own. Get your own pack.

I do think that a lot of my own self-belief and can-do attitude comes from how we were raised by Mum and Dad. We were raised to be the very best versions of ourselves. I have a wonderful Mother- and Father-in-law as well, and I have the best friends in the world. They are my people, and they let me be me. So, for you, surround yourself with the right people and build your own support system if the one nature gave you isn't great.

When I became ill, it was <u>hard</u>. When I recovered, I made a change. It was all about being brave and jumping in. I now help women all over the world, and it is the most incredible experience. I feel like I am doing what I was born to do.

You can too.

I help amazing women create their own online service business and get consistent "high ticket" clients through my online program. Not everyone can afford $10K per month on *Facebook* ads. So, I teach these women how to create their service business and get clients organically, i.e., for free. It is a proven system.

It works.

Did I change course on the way to this point? Of course I did. What I started out with is not what I am doing now, but I listened to the market, and I built what they wanted. Here's what I did when I started out:

I tried to sell a service that few wanted, so I became much more objective and recorded all sales calls and captured all feedback. I documented true pain points and what people actually wanted. I iterated my service and my offer to be what they wanted, and it became easy, not hard. I followed this system to gain high-ticket clients every single day.

If you are serious about creating and growing your online service business and getting consistent, high-ticket clients, schedule your complimentary session with me below"

https://go.oncehub.com/CoursePreviewCall

One client that I work with is an amazing, inspirational lady. She did not believe that she could do it. She had a vague idea of what she wanted to do, but that was it. But she did it. Watching her blossom and seeing her business grow has been so rewarding. I learned that no matter your mindset going into the process, it can be changed, and anything becomes possible. All you have to do is go for it.

I created an amazing online program that helps women every single step of the way on that journey. Strategy matters. Tactics matter. Mindset matters. They are all built into my formula. No stone is left unturned. My program that has helped women just like you all around the world and is called **The High Ticket Formula.**

In the program, we delve deep into the change that is required if you are to become a success. We carry out deep work on niche and life design, and then I bring you through my client journey method so that you can build a business that is systems driven. We work through identifying the market's pulse and organic attraction methods so that you can get consistent, high-ticket clients before you build your offer. We then move on to the build, where we roll our sleeves up and get our hands dirty. We map out your plans and execution framework, and I take you through world-class, organic-sales magic that simply works. Then we push **Go!** on your business and support you as your business takes off.

If you want to find out more about my work, reach out to me via

support@maeveferguson.com

or via *Facebook*, just search "Maeve Ferguson."

I feel so lucky that I have the freedom now to live the life that I want. You can have that too. When our baby arrives, we can do things the way we want, because I am no longer in the corporate rat race. I decide who, when, where and when. I can work from wherever. Whenever. The formula works. It really is the laptop lifestyle and you can have it too, so the life that you are currently dreaming of, can actually become your reality.

So, this is what I know now about the secret to success:

- Do the work
- Niche down tight
- Invest in the right result-based coach
- Surround yourself with the right people
- Create a scalable automated business
- Be consistent
- Sell what people want
- Keep your why in mind

"Believe in your ability to figure it out."

~ Maeve Ferguson

Maeve

Ferguson

Let's do a quick recap so you can grasp the key concepts:

- What do you currently do that clients are not paying high ticket for ($2K+)?

- What do you need to do instead?

- What do you need to do before you build your service?

- What do you need to do right now?

Here are three things that you can do right now, to make things happen in your business.

1. Figure out exactly what your niche wants.

2. Get high ticket clients every single day.

3. Automate.

If you want help with any of these, just send me an email at:

support@maeveferguson.com

About the Author

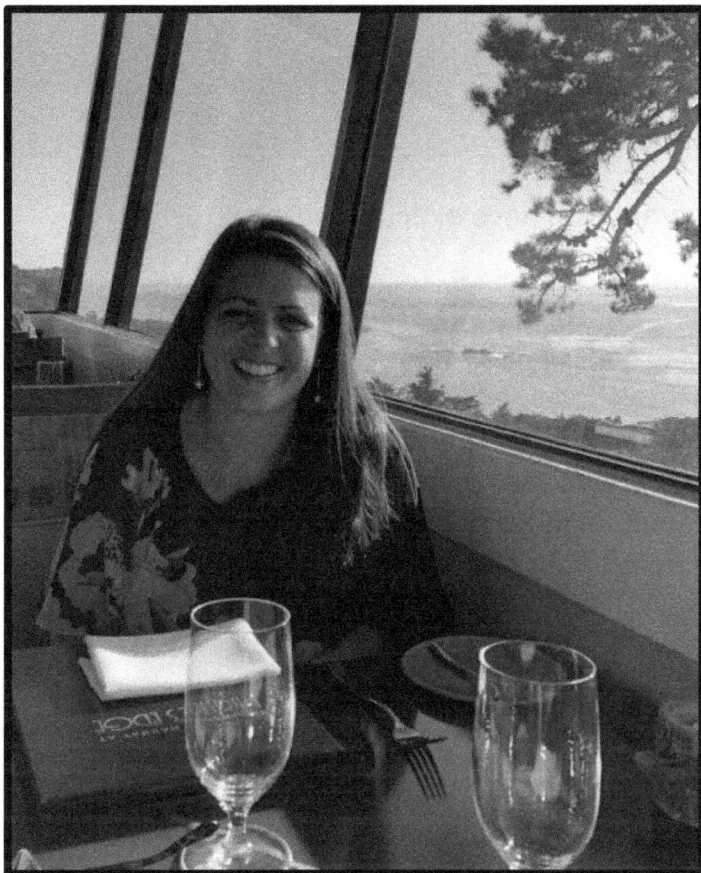

Maeve Ferguson

Business Name: Maeve Ferguson Coaching

Website: www.maeveferguson.com

Email: support@maeveferguson.com

Facebook: https://web.facebook.com/maeve.gormley.5

Instagram: @maevefexecutivecoach

LinkedIn: www.linkedin.com/in/maeveferguson

Service: The High Ticket Formula

Ideal Clients: I work with women around the world who want to create their own online service business and get consistent, high-ticket clients, so they can live life on their own terms.

Colour Your Soul

Maria Fleet
Tattooist and Hypnotherapist, Wales, U.K.

*'Love from your heart; from your soul, because
when you do, great things will come.'*
~ Maria Fleet

The Unthinkable

Do you believe in magic?

Neither did I until three years ago. (This is quite uncanny coming from a family business named 'Abracadabra' – LOL!) I was someone who struggled to watch any fantasy films, as they were so far-fetched. It's funny how your reality can shift, and your consciousness can rise, so much that you're in the process of changing your whole life, the entire 39 years of it. (Even so, I now understand the magic behind the fantasy film or book. I now look on them with a new light).

Always full of self-doubt, a shy, sensitive child, it took a lot of growth for me to be able to tattoo. Stepping out of my comfort zone was necessary. My tattoo clients are like my family. They have helped me reach a level of confidence in my work and helped me believe in myself as a person. I will always be grateful for each and every one who trusted me with their skin; they taught me so much. Thank you. Remember everyone you're in contact with is a lesson or a blessing.

Even though I appeared to have it all – the career and the family – on the inside, I felt something was missing. I felt empty, an inner knowing that there was more. My career is amazing. I am forever grateful, and to this day, I love the people and creating art. But there was an internal feeling that there was more – a desire, a passion for the feeling of true happiness that I was yearning for so much. Being a Cancer star sign, <u>emotion</u> is everything. I must feel at peace with every situation I encounter. I have to live my truth.

A faith sat inside that would stir at times of adversity. A knowing that things will be all right. It was a kind of resilience button that, when the chips were down, provided me a faith would guide me. It was my inner satnav that I knew would carry me through. There were so many signs throughout my younger years guiding me to the next part of the puzzle, and with my creative mind that some may label bi-polar (I got asked this once) it was easy for some people to label me as having a with a mental illness. But disorders don't sit well for me; it's all about flipping the switch. I have a creative mind, and I will use it to create something great.

<u>Believe</u> in yourself. <u>Believe</u> in your path. It is necessary to fend off comments such as *'She needs to seek professional help'* when you know deep in your heart that you're doing all the relevant parts of healing. Healing is messy and confusing, but so worth it.

Always remember, life is a game. We're here to make good, to do good, to be kind and considerate. Life has ups and downs but always look for the beauty in the situation.

Find a positive, but never, never brush over the emotion you feel. We all need to feel these emotions. Sit with them, acknowledge them.

Cry if you need to – like a river running to the sea. Let it out. Talk about it. Be inspired by those around you and get creative. These are my three secrets to a healthy mind.

This is where tattooing saved me. I had all three at my fingertips during the chat where I could be myself and show vulnerability. It satisfied my soul, and we have lots of fun. If you combine this with energy healing, nurturing the soul, meditation, exercise, healthy eating – together, all of this can help you raise your consciousness, lift yourself up to a new energy where you'll have less illness, mentally and physically. You'll be happier and see the world in a new light.

Always remember you have to live your truth. Don't live for others; it's your time. Make it a good one.

This is where I've been for the past two years, bordering on the edge of madness. Is that what Einstein felt like when he discovered the 'secret'? Did he reach the same level and connect with his intuition that led him to great discoveries?

'Intuition is a very powerful thing, more
powerful than intellect.'
~ Albert Einstein

Did his family want to get him help? Maybe so, we'll never know. For me, this path is only the beginning. Where it will lead, I need not know, but you need to have faith – faith in the journey and faith in yourself that will lead you on your Yellow Brick Road to the Emerald City, picking up your heart, courage, and brains on the way. It is faith that will lead you to find your true purpose in life.

The Conflict

My Yellow Brick Road started in 2017.

I felt lost, disharmony and annoyance with the way I wanted to move forward with my life. There was a feeling of needing more out of life, something more that would nurture my soul. I could not put these feelings into words for when I tried, I'd often get misunderstood. People would say something like, '*You're too sensitive*'. People got angry with me for the different way that I'd think. I was afraid of conflict, and I would avoid it at all costs because I had no boundaries. Add to this the feelings I had that I wasn't good enough, plus a language issue where I struggled to find the right words, and this all built up a catalyst of emotion that made me feel anger, resentment, and guilt. There was so much past stuff that I hadn't healed from and I needed the courage to face it head-on, to release these feelings. I knew they couldn't come with me anymore.

There were suicides around me – my young customer, Dan who had an amazing presence, one of life's genuine souls. Such a loss! He could never see his worth. It was so, so sad. Sadness fell on everyone he knew. That day I knew I had to start living for me, not for others, and I also had a burning desire to help kids like Dan in one way or another before it was too late.

I needed to change me, my life, everything. I couldn't carry this feeling any more. I stood connecting with nature and asked myself, '*Why did I feel this way? I wasn't born this way. I was born with love. Where has all this came from?*'

The first thing I did, was to forgive, forgive a stepmother that often would make me feel unloved and disconnected from my father that I love with all my heart. She died 20 years ago. I stood in the field that day and said. 'I forgive you; I will never talk badly of you again.'

From that day on, my life shifted, I'd made the most heart-wrenching decision to leave a family business of 30 plus years because an opportunity for my own place came up. Then, everything fell into place. I had dreams, signs, guiding me to this Yellow Brick Road, and I knew I had to follow it for financial security and a new start. I knew how much this decision would hurt the people I loved, but I had to do it for me and my family. And, I also had an inner knowing that there was more that I didn't know, but I knew I needed more – more adventure, more excitement.

I'd gone stale.

My tattoo shop was born in August 2018, and we called it 'Essentia', meaning 'essence', or 'soul'. This naming came about before I started to open up my psychic gifts. How coincidental? The name had the subheading, 'Tattoos Made with Love', and certainly in the last 10 years or more, I put love and my soul into each one, doing the best I could, trying to better each and every day. I loved the people and the chats. There isn't a job like this anywhere else you get real with people, listening, chatting, and learning. I am truly blessed.

This decision left me feeling shame, guilt, anger all the emotions I needed to heal. So, I started meditating. I got a wonderful life coach, did energy healing, read articles, began to understand who I was, studied hypnotherapy, understood my personality, understood my strengths and my shadow side, and as I lifted, my consciousness lifted. When my intuition rocketed, my psychic strengths grew. As an empath with an INFJ[1] personality, hurting people is the last thing you want to do, but understanding when you have to do things for yourself is an important part of your growth.

I loved more but was also seen as someone who needed help! I could now say, '*I love you*'. I could now hug and chat with random strangers, a confidence that I never had before. It felt so good, so freeing! Does this sound like a mind of madness? I'll let you decide. It was a change, but a change I needed. I needed it to feel strong inside, to know I had this. I could now cope with ever what life threw at me.

My relationships improved. They got rocky, but ultimately they got stronger. The people that were meant to stay did, and some went, but that's okay. You can't take everyone with you on your Yellow Brick Road.

The clutches of madness came, becoming clairaudient[2], hearing a voice to 'heal' people when they were in pain. I questioned my sanity, attended mental health workshops, and gained knowledge. In all this time, I had no time off work. I had the strength to understand what was happening to me. It was my very own spiritual awakening. I lived a life of what I can describe here as in the present, but also my mind would almost feel like it floated up high in a world of soulfulness. It is difficult to describe, combining the spiritual with the physical world is a balance that needs to

---

[1] 'INFJ (introverted, intuitive, feeling, and judging) is one of the 16 personality types identified by the Myers-Briggs Type Indicator (MBTI). Sometimes referred to as the "Advocate" or the "Idealist," people with INFJ personalities are creative, gentle, and caring.' www.wellmind.com.

[2] *Clairaudience* is the capability of receiving an intuitive vocal message from the world of spirits or a higher being. www.kasamba.com.

be fulfilled. I balanced it, running a business, a family, all while going through a massive change in who I was becoming, while combining well-being and a passion for helping others.

This was a very confusing but fascinating time filled with synchronicities and guidance to a future that I am now co-creating. There were special people in my life who came. They believed in me, and they gave me hope in a time of such darkness. I will always be grateful for these people. I had many conversations that seemed coincidental, but in my world, there are no coincidences. They led me to the next part of the puzzle. Piece by piece, the jigsaw started to connect. Each day brought a new dawn, a new chance to be a better person. To love with compassion and see what comes, for whatever it is, is the highest good, and I'm sure that what I want to manifest will come.

Law of attraction at its greatest!

The Breakthrough and Lessons Learned

Understanding the mind has been a breakthrough, where I understood the subconscious doesn't like change. It will try to keep you the same person, repeating old coping mechanisms which no longer serve you.

Knowing that achieving change is harder than staying the same, but it is possible. You can create your own reality. Learning how we react to stress with the fight-or-flight reflex, how, at the time of any stressful incident, you only handled it with what you knew at that time. Learning how with hypnotherapy and NLP, we can reprogram your subconscious to create new belief systems which help you be more positive and live the life you want. We can train this brain to help us rather than hinder us. Understanding your emotions, looking at every angle combining with logic, will lead you to better decisions.

Understanding that helped me release my hold on past childhood experiences, forgive myself and others, and release all attachments that no longer served me. I understood that I was in a constant circle of 'victim' mode. I had no boundaries, and people treated me as they wished, which was sometimes unkind, due to me not being able to confront them. I didn't do well with confrontation. Now, I can hold my own and not allow people to say unkind things. Then there is a mutual respect that comes from grace. Never underestimate what you went through. Each part was relevant for you, and others may go through what you think of as worse trauma, but essentially, it's still trauma, and you need to be healed from it.

- When dealing with others, try to understand their point of view. Understand they have learned behaviours from their past that create their reality.

- Be honest with yourself. Assess your behaviours in a situation and never be afraid to say I'm sorry.

- Always accept your emotions. Sit with them, feel them, and then be gentle on yourself. Don't put them in a box because when the next stress comes along, things could get wild. 😜

- Always believe in yourself. Imagine your life; visualise and let it flow. Work on your personal development stage and good things will come. Believe in the Law of Attraction.

- Get quiet. You know the answers. Enjoy quiet time, meditate, and the answers will come.

- Surround yourself with people who believe in you, your tribe! Inspire each other.

- Accept criticism. Don't react negatively. Take it in and talk it through. Work on how you can be a better version of you, have better relationships, and create a better environment. This sums up spirituality for me.

The Ordinary World

I was born and bred in the village of Cefn Fforest, in the valleys of Wales, in the U.K. Cefn Fforest is a supportive community that encourages everyone to do their best to uplift each other. It's a place where street parties happen for the Queen's Jubilee celebration. Success has been felt in Cefn Fforest, with a world record holder tattooist (my dad) and a champion horse, Dream Alliance, winning the Grand Nationals.

We grew up in a loving home with a big extended family where my dad was a hard-working man, a coalman, who decided to begin tattooing after winning the bingo and buying his first tattoo machine. He had a successful 40-year career. My mam, a loving housewife then factory worker, brought us up with the most love you could ever imagine. At the age of five, I had a few ACEs[3] when my parent's divorced and I endured bullying at school for many years. This became a reoccurring pattern that then, I didn't understand what I needed to do to stop it. My stepfather has been amazing. He listens to my dreams, visions, and we have the best chats. My second stepmother brings out the love in my dad, and forever I'll be grateful for that. I have three brothers, all whom I love dearly.

Overall, I have a loving family who sometimes struggle

---

[3] 'ACE' is an acronym for 'adverse childhood experience'.

to understand me, but support and love me in the best way they can.

I now have my own sensitive family. The three of us are all sensitive souls. We understand what we need at the right time. Understanding my daughter's needs and analysing my sensitivities, I can see what she needs to flourish as a sensitive soul in a world that can so easily seem dark, depending on which way you look at it. She teaches me patience and encourages me to love harder. Together, we will continue to support each other, and a brighter future will be had.

I promise her that.

As a child, I would always dream about my future. I was determined to have a good career. At the age of seven, I did my first tattoo, and the rest is history. Now, I sit here and look at all those memories fondly, appreciate what they have given me, and now it's time to create a new part of me. This new chapter hasn't quite formed yet, and it's been confusing and uplifting at times, trying to piece together what it is showing me. I've been guided through various parts, such as shamanism, hypnotherapy, mental health, and healing. So, I believe it wants me to create a building dedicated to helping people while transitioning from tattooing into this new part of my Yellow Brick Road.

Wish me well 🖤

The Drama

While I transitioned from shop to shop, I hit a great darkness, maybe the 'dark night of the soul'. I had to try to continue to work through it while supporting my family and continue to heal my past which was tainted with the emotional abuse of bullying I encountered as a child. I had to try to understand these strong psychic connections. I thought I'd just go to the new studio and tattoo for the next 15 years, but after I'd been in there just a month, a new feeling washed over me and left me with the knowledge that I needed more. I started to understand why I had been led to this calming environment in this building called the 'Old Doctors Surgery'. It was to help people.

There were signs everywhere, left, right, and centre, leading me to this new path. Up until now, I'd been on a path that didn't fit with me all my life, and that's where that feeling of needing 'something more' had come from. I'd been trying to be someone who I was not. Materialism was not the answer. My soul needed nurturing. The more events I went on, such as an Ayahuasca conference and a UFO conference, and the more I met people that were of my tribe, the more it excited me. The more experiences like meditation weekends and Gong Baths, the more I connected pieces of my past together. I loved every part of this.

It felt so right.

The last six months of being at my old studio taught me patience and timing. I had no time off through a time of dark thoughts. My new shop had a flood of water from the bad weather, and I reacted differently than the old me would have. That day I knew I'd changed. It was knowing that this was something that would work out. I was on the right path. I got in my car to phone the insurance, and the clock showed it was 11:11; I knew then everything would all be all right. The faith was there.

I created some of the best tattoos during this struggle, as something I've learnt is that through adversity and people's negative behaviours gives me fire, fire to rise like a phoenix where the determination is at its strongest to achieve, achieve whatever it takes to make me happy. I understood the impact of my decision, looked at their points of view, apologised if necessary, but sometimes in life, we need to shake things up, in order not to dip into the anxiety and depression that you'll feel if you don't move forward. Even though it hurts at the time, do it with love and integrity, and know that things will come good in the end.

The Call to Action

Are you wondering how hypnotherapy came onto my path? I'll tell you how one of my first synchronicities made me take notice.

Walking my dog one morning in early August 2018, I met a lady in the park. She lived in my village, but I had never seen her before. Her dog had the same name as my daughter. Coincidence one! Walking around, we chatted. I got vulnerable and said, *'I feel there's something else I need to do'*.

She said 'Do it! I did'. She went on to explain her change into hypnotherapy. I stood there and the energy impulses around my head were massive, something I've never experienced. Head tingles happen when you meet someone relevant on your path, but this was bigger and more intense. I questioned this as I went home and wondered what this was showing me.

I found a Sunday hypnotherapy course that met once a month, and the rest is history. I've met wonderful people there who I'm sure we'll be friends for life – my tribe! There have been so many people who've helped me through their conversations. Some that are my mentors. For these, I am so grateful.

The synchronicities I have had have been so many, I'd need to write another book to even begin to cover them all.

The Growth and Brightness of the Future

As I sit here and write way too many words, LOL, I hope for a wonderful glow of well being for myself and my family. I hope for pure love and excitement that will help them live a life with purpose. This path I'm on is creative. It's different to the old me where I needed to control every aspect. Freedom feels so good.

But I also understand that we have responsibilities, a life that is destined to help people. I hope to show the younger generation that there are many paths, and you don't need to stay on the same as everyone else. When feelings of anxiety set in, they are showing you that you need to move. Move on try something new, and you'll find something that excites your soul where you don't feel tired anymore because each day is a blessing.

Have you ever experienced that tired feeling but have slept eight hours solid? That is your soul calling; it needs nourishing.

After I've finished my hypnotherapy, I hope to continue to study both sides – the ancient methods, such as shamanism, combined with the college path. I'm sure my efforts will be guided in what it's meant to be, a sanctuary to help people through their challenges through hypnosis and other methods. I wish to continue to grow our community wellbeing group, Karuna Kinnect, with seven of my wonderful volunteers and help as many people as we can, both adults and youth.

So, for now, I will continue to tattoo and work tirelessly to build the other side of my business up in order to make a difference.

The Reward

As this journey continues, I wish for financial security to be able to live freer so that I can spend more time with my family, eat better, have time to do yoga every day, and continue my spiritual practice. I want to be able to do all these things while bringing light to other people's lives through my business and building a better community where everyone starts to feel more lifted.

My personal goal is to take my tribe of three around the world, meeting other tribes, experiencing their cultures, talking to strangers that uplift you with their way of life conversations that ignite your soul. I want to do all this while documenting it. Imagine that! That has to be travelling at its best for a child like mine who works with her creativity, who goes into school and asks her teachers their star signs (she melts my heart) rather than their academic credentials. I really think travelling this way would help her grow, to see the world with new eyes.

It would be a different way of living.

The Wisdom

- Trust your gut; you know the answers.
- Combine the physical reality with the non-physical to make a decision.
- Always be honest with the utmost integrity.

- There are only two things you can control – what you say and how you react. Everything else will just happen.

- Keep dreaming, take action with small steps, and it will come.

'Every task, complete it with love in your heart,
try your best, and good will follow. Believe'.

~ Maria Fleet

About the Author

Maria Fleet is an award-winning tattoo artist who has developed a love for the mind by sitting with people and colouring them in! She is an up and coming hypnotherapist, who loves all things 'energy' and is fascinated by the unknown! She has big dreams and visions for a better future. A community of love must be built first before the world can change, and all healing starts within. Raising the vibrations of a man or woman must start first, then we will see a world where we're all able to manifest using the new energy of 2020.

Maria is the mother to an amazing, intuitive child who sees the good in everything, and started her on this journey. A cat who is super fluffy and the best-behaved chihuahua in the world!

She likes to call herself a passionate community teacher, uplifting the community with her group Karuna Kinnect which practices mindfulness from the soul ♥

She also volunteers as a trustee with 'Inside Out Cymru', a mental health charity in Wales.

Maria is always ready for an adventure, living a life where she can get to be free, and travelling with peace and balance in her heart.

Be well!

Maria Fleet

Business Name: Essentia

Website: www.essentiatattoo.co.uk

Facebook:
Essentia Tattoo Studio
https://web.facebook.com/mariafleettattoo/

Essentia Serenity
https://web.facebook.com/essentiacomplementaryandalter
nativetherapy/

Karuna Kinnect
https://web.facebook.com/groups/952232185121087/

Instagram: essentia.tattoo studio / essentiaserenity

Services: We are a creative environment where we offer tattooing and piercing combined with self-care, energy healing, intuitive massage, hypnosis, and counselling.

Ideal Client: All people of all ages and gender who want to understand their emotions.

Trust Your Intuition

Michael Pinto
Business Consultant, Germany

"When your mind is preventing you to try it, but your gut may be telling you the contrary, just give it a try. Don't overthink it."

~ Michael Pinto

Meaning and Purpose

I remember it like it was yesterday. I was on the way home. It was mid-summer '98 in France and very hot. I was wearing an old Michael Jordan t-shirt and listening to Notorious BIG on my old Walkman. I was happy. At that time, my plan was just like everyone's plan at my age. In a few weeks, I would study in France, namely law, what my parents advised me to study. I would live in my own flat and finally leave my parent's house because I couldn't bear it any longer over there. Actually, it sounds like I had everything well planned to begin my own "adult life," didn't it?

Back home, everything suddenly changed. I had received a letter from the French Army. I was actually informed that I was drafted into army service. And even worse, I'd have to go to a French garrison in Germany. I didn't know yet exactly where the garrison was located, and I didn't want to know.

This picture of life made no sense at all and was quite strange like the tricks life sometimes plays on you. At this point of my story, you probably don't know what I'm talking about, but please read further to understand what I mean!

At that time, I was making a lot of music in the hip-hop scene. For me, making music was everything in my life (more about this later). A few days later, I'd been invited by a friend of mine to make a trip to a hip-hop festival in Trier, Germany. And – here it comes – finally, I met a French guy there, Laurent, who was active in the hip-hop scene in Trier, and he had lived there for 20 years. I have to say that Laurent had a really good band (French/German rap combo) which was slowly gaining success in the region. Laurent is a former French soldier, so I told him also my dilemma with the French army, and he told me that my garrison was only 15 minutes away from Trier.

What a coincidence! Suddenly, all my new situation has made sense! Do you follow me?

"Nothing happens without meaning and purpose."

Stick to Your Gut – Round 1

A couple of weeks later, I began my military service in Germany. As the weeks passed by and in my spare time, I met in Trier with some inspiring, creative people with similar interests. I then became a member of Laurent's band, and we had already nice gigs. Looking back, I've felt really comfortable, and It was so cool over there, that I spent a lot of weekends there instead of spending my free time back home in France!

During my military service, I've was ordered to participate in a military operation in Bosnia – so far so good, but then I was sent to the conflict in Kosovo. I almost died out there due to an anti-personal mine.

On my return, it was impossible to ignore that a lot of things has changed in my life. What should you feel after spending five months in a former war zone? Furthermore, our band had signed a record deal during my absence with a major U.S. label.

All those things really struck me deep in my gut. I didn't feel I could implement my plan in France. I was finally toying with the idea, "*Should I consider emigrating to Trier?*"

My gut feeling said, "Yes, take the risk for a change!"

One morning, at the beginning of September '99 and only with what I could fit in the back of my small French car, I moved to Germany.

Faith and Hope

First of all, you need to know that I come from a very humble family. My parents have never supported me, and we didn't have a good relationship at all.

At the beginning in Germany, I only had a bed and a roof over my head in one friend's flat (Laurent's). I had little money at my disposal, was only a high school graduate, and really spoke very little German! Whatever, I was sure I would manage it.

But because of all that, the beginning was really bumpy.

I found out a couple of weeks later that without the language skills, I would be unable to accomplish much there. I have to study hard to learn the German language for as much as six to eight hours every damn day! Okay? But I had somehow to earn money in order to survive!

It is important to note that the record deal should only cover the production of some "single EPs," so we didn't hit the jackpot, and every member needed to earn some money on the side.

So, what else could I do but to get a job and reduce the time I should have spent studying German?

From that moment on, many people in France and Germany often told me that I could not make it. That, it would be unrealistic to believe I could get over both the language financial barriers. Motivating words sound completely different.

I became disillusioned with friends and relatives whom I used to value and respect, but I really had to ask myself "Should I stay, or should I return to France?" Maybe I was somewhat naïve to believe and trust in my gut.

Despite many suggestions that I return to France, I decided to take a mini-job in a fast-food restaurant to keep my head above water.

Looking back, once again, I must insist on the fact that nothing made sense for anybody within my circle of friends and my relatives. There were a lot of misunderstandings and demotivating factors, and it was a sad period of time for all of us.

Finally, I was the only person who thought I could make it!

A couple of months later, after a change of employer, I was actually allowed to work for an international sports shoes and accessories supplier. I was finally moving in the right direction: more money and better language skills. That did me good after all the discouragement and stupid comments because looking back. I was really knocked back for six months by these setbacks. But now, I had also managed, within just a few months, to be promoted to assistant manager!

"Life is about finding joy and motivation in your own faith and hope, your own actions, results and experiences and to reward yourself periodically in everyday life."

But all these small successes were no longer sufficient. I had already big goals and visions that were swirling around in my head, which should be achieved as soon as possible.

Stick to your gut – Round 2

When I was 23 years old, I decided to apply for a job in Luxembourg, for which I was definitely under-qualified, but I did it once again based on my gut feeling!

"When your mind is preventing you to try it, but your gut may be telling you the contrary, just give it a try. Don't overthink it."

There was nothing positive for a while. What a setback, but I didn't want to give up. After a lot of applications, what had seemed like over a 100, I finally received a positive response!

How could you repeat this?

Develop and Use your Best Skills to Make it Happen…

1. …by knowing about your own capabilities;
2. …by picking up the best of the list, and finally;
3. …by bringing and proving it as often as possible!

High-income skills – these are one of the keys to success!

So, I had found out my own skills: quick understanding and perception, strong language skills as well. I know that I was saved and moved another step up to a higher standard of life.

I started out as a junior product manager at a Luxembourg building company group. At the age of 24, I could show my competencies once again as a junior key-account manager in the same company group.

There were many times I wanted to give up, but I always believed in myself.

Where others see problems, I see opportunities. It's all matter of your perspective and your own interpretation of your own situation.

What saddened me the most was that while I earned good money, Luxemburg is well known for that, I was neither a happy person nor in harmony with myself.

"Love is love and money is money, money won't make you happy, but when you are happy you are likely to get money which will keep you happy."

Musical Harmony and Scale

With a strong interest for entrepreneurship, some good skills and some talent in hip-hop music (as an MC and DJ and then later as a music producer / artist manager), I registered my first commercial business in the music industry. It was at the beginning of 2000. We were signed by a major label at that time.

Stick to Your Gut – Round 3

In 2005, I quit my well-paid job in Luxemburg based on my gut feeling and founded another company in music management and production. I was 26 years old. It was at that time the right decision because I'd made it so far in the music industry with the former business dealings.

As you already know, my band had a record deal, a lot of performances at big concerts and festivals, and then some really good projects with internationally renowned artists at an international level. No one expected it, but I've always believed it would happen, and that one of the reasons why it all worked out.

After her studies in 2006, my partner in life wanted to move back to Hannover in order to be near her family and to find a challenging job over there. So, I had to make a decision, and I went with her for love, following my gut feeling as usual. Then, after nearly three years of operations and some beautiful experiences with the management of greats artists, I utterly failed in this tough industry and closed down this business!

"Do everything to develop at first the best version of what you got as a human being and as a company as well!"

But looking back, it was a beautiful time, and I had learned a lot. I was 30 years old and ready to make a lateral move into the consulting industry.

…and, as desired, I still will be with my beautiful partner in life, and we are now parents of a beautiful three-year-old son!

Business and Personal Growth

And if I told you that after all you already have learned from my story, I found a better way to my own success?

Just read on. You will learn how I made it!

Today, I am a successful entrepreneur, and I deliver my expertise in business consulting at an international level. You probably wondering how I reached such a high level of expertise with my background, and let me tell you, that's a legitimate question!

When someone asks me how I arrived at this stage, I simply tell them that I always have followed my gut feeling, and then I've taken the required steps in order to be successful.

Naturally, my notable success was not only about taking some decisions, but from the process perspective, it is incredibly important to trigger such an event. So many companies are not making progress just because of a lack of decision-making competencies. In my opinion, it's all about making decisions quickly and acting flexibly. For my part, I've learned to decide quickly and react as fast as possible in all circumstances. How? Just by practising it as often as possible and by getting more and more self-confidence.

There are always only two possibilities in every action: either you make it, or you learn a life's lesson from it.

Of course, such decisions have some degree of risk.

My advice to you is:

1. In order to reach your goal and objectives, you have to know where you want to go and how you can get there.

2. It's all about having a strong "why" behind your ambitious vision and getting a clear picture of your "how".

You probably know that many people don't know where they stand, and sometimes, they also don't know where they intend to go. Maybe you might be one of these people. and let me tell you, by the way, that it's okay! But it's your fault if changes don't occur. And why is it so important? Just because it's the only way to allow you as well to exceed yourself again and again!

But let's get back to my own exponential growth.

As previously mentioned, I'm a business consultant. I deliver my expertise in French, German and, of course, English as well.

Today I help ParentPreneurs (parents + entrepreneurs) to boost their business and optimize their performance (triple their turnover) to relieve stress and frustration and to ensure time and a better future for their children.

It takes a minimum of three months[4] to bring you to the next level and to improve and strengthen your position in the market. I will help you as well to become a better version of yourself!

But you still have the same question: how did I reach such a high level of expertise with my background?

And now comes the best.

Back then, in 2008, when my life had turned a new corner, I've started as a career-changer in the consulting business at a small German consulting firm. But now, you are probably wondering as well how on earth I got to it? Thinking back, I've to laugh about it, because this has simply happened. Just to make it clearer, it happened during a birthday party for a friend of my partner in life. I got one beer from a guy, and we're having a conversation which went so well that I finally received from him an extremely interesting career opportunity in a consulting business. Between you and me, at that time, I didn't know what I'd got myself into, but once again, I've relied on my gut feeling.

Concerning the expected hard skills, I really started from nothing. As you already know, I didn't study, and to become a consultant without a real good CV and degree; it's almost impossible. In the beginning, I've to acquire the knowledge and skills I lacked while working on the projects. The years 2008 and 2009 were certainly not easy years for me. It was actually the worst times of my entire life. Forty-hour

---

[4] FYI: I'm accompanying my clients until the predefined goals are accomplished!

workweeks on top travelling times of several hours per week to try to not only work but lessen my deficiencies.

My situation/ decision led me out of my "comfort zone" for a while, but also led me to success in such a way.

In 2010, I first put my own team together. In 2012, I'd been nominated as a shareholder and member of the board. At that moment, I made the goal of the company my own goal, namely the to contribute to the healthy growth of this medium-sized consulting firm into an international company group. Now, my former partners and I have achieved that! We had over 250 employees worldwide in 2017, even though we were under 20 employees in 2008.

This small-sized company has become an international company group specialized in management and IT-consultancy with around about 250 employees working in more than seven subsidiaries worldwide, including an investment and real-estate firm. We were a German company group with a total annual turnover on the order of 25 million euros in 2018.

This exponential company growth has ensured my own growth as well!

I've delivered my expertise into several industries, the financial sector, home loan savings, energy industry, retail, wholesale engineering, etc., in more than 15 countries all over Europe. Finally, my life has completely changed over just nine years in the consulting business. It was my own personal exponential growth, and I am proud and happy at the same time.

My Advice to You

*"Success is like hunted species – if you can't see it, it can't
see you. It's only a matter of your own feelings and
thoughts. The focus is not on one or the other but on both!"*

Less is More

My father passed away from a heart attack in 2015. Several
weeks later, I've found out that I would become a father for
the first time in my life. This was a bitter setback concerning
my father and great news concerning my son.

That's why I've decided to take such measures to adapt
my life and future to my new situation. At that time, I had a
five to six-day workweek travelling through Europe and was
rarely at home during the week. Relying once again on my
gut feeling, I decided to quit my job as a shareholder and
member of the executive board. My goal was to create my
own business by delivering my business consulting
expertise as an "online service." I really wanted to be at
home more often and to be around for my son and my
partner in life!

It took some time to reach the period of notice and the
end of my partnership, but finally, I started my current
business in 2018. It was, once again, the right decision.

If you want to find out more about my business
consulting services, just email me at…

mail@michaelpintoconsult.com

…and we'll have a chat or connect with me on *Facebook*
at…

web.facebook.com/michael.pinto.9250

…or on *LinkedIn* at…

www.linkedin.com/in/michael-pinto

I'm now scaling my businesses to seven figures and beyond (relying on my gut feeling, LOL 😊). I'm excited to be working on big projects right now in the French and German market as well. Viewed from a mid-term perspective, I will help you build the foundation necessary to ensure your own business success by ensuring you a really good entrepreneurial education.

The access to success should be accessible, regardless of your social background.

Let me give you once again a short summary of my best advice:

1. Nothing happens without meaning and purpose. React (analyze and act) to every sign and feeling to become the master of your own universe!

2. Stick to your guts and do something from your personal story and experience, because this shit is unique.

3. Life (business and private) is about finding joy and motivation in your own faith and hope, your own actions, results and experiences, and to reward yourself periodically in everyday life.

4. Find out your own high-income skills and showcase your capabilities as much as you can.

5. Think positive and always relate to solution-oriented thinking and acting, because everything else is bullshit.

6. Know where you are right now and where you want to go. It's all about having a strong "why" behind your real ambitious vision and getting a clear picture of your "how."

7. Do not underestimate the power of a regular analysis of your current situation and the necessary changes to stay on course.

8. Always think big enough. It starts when you think it's too crazy!

9. Get the best out of what you have before trying to get or invent something new.

10. Always act to convince everyone emotionally as well as intellectually, intuitively as well as rationally.

"If there were a way to make things better for my own person, I would do it the same way but much faster."

~ Michael Pinto

Love and blessings,

Success Actions

Here are three success actions that you can take right now to boost your business:

1. Write down your direction for the next three months, six months and one year.

2. Realize a SWOT[5] analysis and use the results to define your main three or four goals.

3. Break each main goal down into some important actions and create an action plan.

If you need some help you can contact me at:

mail@michaelpintoconsult.com

---

[5] SWOT analysis is a strategic planning technique used to help a person or organization identify strengths, weaknesses, opportunities, and threats related to business competition or project planning.

About the Author

Mike Pinto was born and raised in France and grew up in a pretty humble background. He is now has been living as an ex-pat in Germany for 20 years. He's 41 years old, in a long-term relationship with his life partner, and the father of a wonderful little son.

He loves beautiful cars, good music, and good conversations!

He has now been acting as a business consultant and mentor for over 12 years and as an entrepreneur/manager for over 18 years.

He's started really early on in his career to manage an international customer portfolio and big projects with the sole aim to increase their productivity and to improve their market situation. In 2018, He opened his own business consulting firm.

Today, he helps *Parent*Preneurs (which is a name that

combines parents+entrepreneurs) to boost their business and optimize their performance, to relieve stress and frustration, and to ensure more time for them at home and a better future for their children.

Business Name: Michael Pinto Consult

Website: https://michaelpintoconsult.com/en/

Email: mail@michaelpintoconsult.com

Facebook: https://www.facebook.com/michael.pinto.9250

Instagram:
   https://www.instagram.com/michael_pinto_consult/

LinkedIn: https://www.linkedin.com/in/michael-pinto/

Products/Services:

1. _Parent_preneur in Gold: As an experienced business consultant, I help _Parent_Preneurs (parent + entrepreneur) to boost their business in a minimum of three months by optimizing their performance (triple your turnover), by relieving stress and frustration, and by ensuring them more time with their family and a better future for their children.

2. Exceed Yourself: As an experienced sparring partner, I offer business owners training in some of the ways together (minimum 12 months) to overcome their current challenges on their way to their ultimate success.

3. Finding Your Own Ultimate Success: As an experienced business consultant, I offer business owners to define within 30 days their ultimate success goals and to plan the way to achieve them.

Ideal Clients: Business Owners, _Parent_Preneurs (in English, French, and German languages)

Life is Full of Opportunities

Michelle Mehta
Teen Confidence Coach, USA

"Always keep your eyes, ears, and heart open, as you will never know what or when the next opportunity is going to be knocking on your door!"

~ Michelle Mehta

The Unthinkable

If I told you I could never succeed in Corporate America, would you believe me? If I told you that I paved my own career path, would you believe me?

When I was 20 years old, I dreamt that I wanted to be in a management position by 25, making a six-figure income, getting ready to be married by 27, and being a mom by 30. When I turned 22, I quickly realized that my dreams were not going to go as planned. I was being held back by the baggage of too many bad management styles that were following me around. Until I did something drastic, my goals were not going to be achieved. All of my peers were having "success" stories of finding their dream jobs, getting promoted to management positions, getting married, having kids, and here I was living a life of confusion, failure, and lack of confidence.

My dating life sucked, with bad dates after bad dates, and meeting people that were not aligned with my purpose and passion in life. My career never took off as planned because I was doing everything that looked good for everyone else, and yet it was not helping me live up to my true potential. I had only one option, and that was to own up to the fact that I was different and reset my goals based on my own happiness. I realized I needed to pave the pathway to what success looked and felt like for me and no one else.

There I was in 2009, working as an intern at a Fortune 500 Investment Firm making telemarketing calls to invite prospects for a complimentary breakfast, lunch, or dinner seminars. It was one of the best times of my life, as I was learning the power of not feeling rejected as people were hanging up on me and told me to never call again. I also learned the skill of persistence.

Every single month I would follow-up with people to see if they were able to make it to a seminar, and every time I would always exceed the capacity of attendees at the monthly seminars.

Then one day, I was doing a routine call, and I happened to have a prospect become a client after following up with him for six months straight. This client was very special because he was a prominent wealthy client and had $1 million dollars to invest during a time when no one else was investing since the market had recently crashed. My managers' quarterly call was to bring in $250,000 of investment, and here I was bringing a client with $1 million dollars exceeding her quarterly call by four times. She decided to give me a reward for my hard work and gave me a $10.00 gift certificate to Starbucks.

I felt like that "reward" was a dagger in my stomach as

my own self-worth was shot to the ground. I could not believe that despite all my hard work, this was the reward I got. I immediately put in my two weeks' notice and waited for the next big opportunity to knock on my door.

I got the opportunity to work as an intern in a Fortune 500 Life Insurance Company through one of my uncle's contacts. I was the first intern this agency had ever hired. I loved what I was doing being a back-end support staff for the agents and learning all the tools to help clients manage finances and money better. As I continued to learn and complete my degree at Cal State Fullerton, I got an opportunity to work full-time, and they recruited me as a life insurance agent, offering me a job right out of college. I was one of the very few students who got to enter Corporate America a day after they graduated from college. Life was very nice and beautiful, until one day my entire team vanished, and their positions were terminated. I had no support around me and decided to go find a new opportunity in the banking industry in 2012.

The Drama

As soon as I entered one of the top banking corporations as a personal banker, I got the shock of my life. I was in a four-week training program where the existing employees who were training for their new position were complaining about how bad their jobs were and were warning us that it is going to be super-challenging once you enter the branch. I ignored their warnings and managed to do my best.

I got to my branch in February and learned the systems and got to know my team members. Then, one fine day in April, my branch underwent an investigation with the store manager and two other personal bankers. My worst fear had reared its ugly head. As a result of that investigation, I became the only personal banker and the most experienced personal banker, even though I had only been there for two months. As time progressed in the branch, I had the highest customer service rating in the entire branch, went through eight different store and service managers, and was told negative things about my sales performance because I decided not to hurt my existing customers by opening accounts they did not need.

In 2013, I was super excited to join the second largest staffing organization in the world. I got to be trained in Phoenix, Arizona for what they told me was going to be six weeks long, and then I will have the opportunity to work in the Irvine, California location. The first week of training was quite unusual as I was the only person from California in this training and we started with 20 people on Monday. By Friday afternoon, they had laid off nine people. I was shocked to see people get laid off during training. Who really does that? Sure enough, I also had a feeling my time was going to come, and it did. I was laid off during the third week of training and was told my excellent customer service skills that I had gained from the banking corporation not only would not help me in this position but would instead hurt me. Really, who fires people for having a great customer service skill set? Apparently, I thought, it is only me that goes through something that drastic.

Once again, I felt like I was confused, broken, and did not matter.

I gathered all the strength and said, "*Thank you,*" to the second-largest staffing corporation, "*I am going to the largest staffing corporation in the world.*" I then quickly nailed another wonderful opportunity working for the largest staffing corporation in the world. I was a talent sourcer and searched for resumes and interviewed IT professionals. This company promised a three-phased program, each phase was going to be 90-120 days. I finished the first phase in 45 days and immediately entered phase two. On my 94th day, I once again got the bad news that I had been terminated. This time the reason was that they could no longer afford me since their sales dropped because of bad placements.

I was once again in shock! How can anyone experience two layoffs within a short span of six months, under the age of 25?

The Turning Point

I did not know what to do. I was lost and miserable and gave up on Corporate America until my amazing family came to my rescue. They gave me the opportunity to work full-time in their business and even started a brand new division for me to learn and run. At the same time, I decided to learn more about a coaching career and completed the certification in 2018.

In 2018, my father decided to sell his business to a Fortune 500 Company, and all of the employees were transferred to the new company. On October 30, I got the best news of my life; I got to be an internal coach, as I got the opportunity to coach one of the managers. Unfortunately, this moment of my life was extremely short-lived. A few hours after completing the paperwork for my client, the vice president came into the office with my direct manager and terminated my position.

That became the worst news of my life.

The internal coaching agreement was immediately

transitioned out to be an <u>external</u> coaching agreement, where I actually got paid for my services. This whole day was like a dream that had come true and was now crashed into a million tiny pieces.

The very next day, I made a decision to become a full-time coach and immediately hired a business coach to start coaching me on November 1. My dream career of my life was now officially launched not knowing who, what, when, where, and how I was going to make it. I just knew <u>why</u> I needed to do it and was prepared to do whatever it took to make it work and truly last a lifetime.

My parents were extremely disappointed that I could not succeed in the traditional route. They were hurt and sad that I had this type of journey in Corporate America. They did not want me to give up and continued to push me to go back into Corporate America, even though I knew that taking the path of entrepreneurship was my ideal path to success, gaining a six-figure income, establishing financial freedom, and finding ultimate happiness.

The Breakthrough and Lessons Learned

I believed in myself and was confident I could create the life I always wanted. I embraced my strengths and weaknesses. I created my dream career and truly understood what it feels like to be happy from within. I learned to pave my own path authentically, and the opportunities for success became endless.

One of the biggest lessons that I learned was during a time when I hired a counselor and I knew that I wanted to give up working for a corporation. Having a counselor in my life helped me to discover my own strengths and weaknesses better and find careers that matched my personality. I also learned to fully express myself without being judged and having biased opinions.

The second biggest lesson I learned was to hire a life coach, as my life coach built upon what my counselor had shared with me about my life and helped me create a plan for where I wanted to go in building a stronger and loving relationship with my own self. I had never taken the time to fully understand myself and my inner beauty. I was always focused on others and working with a life coach helped me to appreciate who I am inside and out.

The third biggest lesson that I learned was turning towards spirituality. I knew that I was lost, and the only way that I could find myself was if I leaned into the power within myself. One of my friends introduced me to a Buddhist mantra, "Nam Myoho Renge Kyo," in 2014. I started chanting "Nam Myoho Renge Kyo," and I immediately started feeling better by seeing positive changes in my life as my relationships with my family and friends got better, and I started to believe in myself, even at times when I wanted to give up. If I had not learned about this mantra, I would not have been the warrior that I am today.

There are times that I wanted to give up in life and having the support from my family despite our differences is what always kept me going and growing. I always remember to do my best, as that is the best I could always do no matter what the circumstances were and can be.

The Ordinary World

I was the firstborn in my family outside of India and was raised with a mix of American and Indian values. I grew up with a tremendous amount of love and have always been surrounded by an extended family of at least 40 members within a 10-mile radius. Having these 40 members all around me, allowed me to have six moms and six dads, not including my own parents. Even to this day, anytime I visit my uncles' and aunts' places, I feel like I am their firstborn, even though they have kids of their own. I grew up with the maximum amount of advice and support compared to my cousins as I felt the bond of a friendship rather than an elder family member.

I went to three elementary schools, one middle school, two different high schools, and attended one major university. I knew there was a reason that I was different. My parents are Indian, and I was the firstborn in my family not to have an Indian name, causing people to be curious as to why I do not have an Indian name and questioning me about what my real name is, and if my name is for real. My parents wanted me to be unique and loved the name Michelle, and I am super grateful for it as it makes it really easy to spell the name for restaurant reservations.

When I was in college, my friends would talk about parties they were attending and would experience underage drinking. I remember telling them Monday morning that I had a blast attending house parties. These house parties were with 40 of my family members, and we would be divided into three groups of dads, moms, and kids. All the dads would be hanging out in the backyard, the moms would be in the living room and the kitchen, and us kids would hang out upstairs watching a movie or playing X-Box. My cousins and I would talk about the things that were happening in school, typical boy-girl dramas.

My parents believed in an open house policy. Every weekend we would have at least one or two families for breakfast, lunch, or dinner, and once a month we would have 40 people over. Being the oldest cousin, my cousins always looked up to me and saw me as their role model.

Going to a local college, allowed me to bond with my cousins even more and created a support system of always being there no matter what. My cousins moved away to college, and they knew they could always count on me, and I continued to be there for them time again and again. It was a beautiful feeling growing up with my cousins and having our own, sober house parties.

I currently live at home with my grandmother, my parents, and my sister in California.

The Downfall

I was bullied in middle school for giving hugs to my friends over and over again. I always had a difficult time expressing myself and showed expressing my love for people through hugs. My friends at that time were not open to me hugging them, were always making fun of me, and made me feel really insecure about who I was.

I grew up with a lot of adults in the house and always was drawn to people who were older to me. I did not like the way my friends were treating me, so instead of hanging out with them, I would go the custodian to see if I could get a trash bag, and I would pick up trash as a reward to get a front-of-the-line lunch pass. It was one of the ways I would spend my lunch breaks so I would not have to get bullied. There were times when I would spend my time during the lunch breaks talking to the principal and the assistant principal about their next vacation plans. I got to build a really strong relationship with the principal and to this day, we are still friends and are able to spend time together.

These insecurities were just the beginning. As I got older and started interning, I realized why I was not able to stand up for myself and just give up. I had multiple opportunities in my career and relationships to feel even less about myself and had lost faith to rise up against the challenges. After taking the Landmark Education Forum in 2010, I realized what I was doing and started to appreciate and love myself more. In 2013, I started working with a counselor and learned what it was like to own who I am and be grateful for the environment that I was raised in.

The Call to Action

One day, I was at a volunteer event volunteering, and when one of the volunteers asked me about my passion, I responded by saying, "*I love helping people.*" He told me if I had ever thought about being a life coach, and I responded with, "*No, I have not.*" He told me I should talk to his daughter, as she is a life coach and loves her career. I spoke to his daughter, and immediately after hanging up the phone with her, I decided to take my first coaching class with Co-Active Training Institute. After completing the first class, I knew that this was my calling and the missing piece of the puzzle of my life had been found.

After the coaching class ended, I realized that I had been coaching my friends for many years already without even knowing it, as I did not know at that time that it was called "coaching." I would always give my friends relationship advice and try to inspire and motivate them to be and feel better about themselves. I even helped one of my friends come out of depression, not even realizing that I was coaching him. When the coaching class ended, they told us, "*Congratulations! You are now a coach. You can go ahead and start charging people.*" It felt extremely natural to me to go out and start implementing the coaching tools without even thinking.

The coaching tools that I continued to learn helped me be passionate about work for the first time in my life. I realized that I got to help people without being a product pusher. I got to set the terms of the coaching sessions and really help my clients win.

It took me three years to complete the five coaching classes, as I wanted to really master the learning from the course work. In 2018, I enrolled in the six-month coaching certification program. What should have taken one year to complete was, for me, a three-year plan, taking about one to two classes a year. I realized that I was in no rush to see what the next steps were as I wanted to feel confident in what I was learning. One of the biggest challenges that I faced was that the majority of Indian people do not invest in personal development, and here I was immersed in personal development. It was challenging to talk to my friends and family as to why I was going down this path, and I knew that I had to go down this path as my soul lit up with every coaching conversation I was creating and learning about day-in and day-out.

The Key Ingredients

A key ingredient for me is go believe in myself enough to know that I am always surrounded by opportunities taking me to the next level. I had at least 15 coaches on *Facebook* personally reach out to me asking me to join their programs, and most of the time I have said "*Yes*" to the services they were offering because I knew that there was a reason why I needed to be connected with them. It was a sign from the universe saying, "*Yes, they will help you get to your next level.*" I knew that I wanted to build a coaching business with a rock-solid foundation and did not want to figure it out on my own. I had dedicated my first year of business to learn all the things I needed to learn to create the strongest foundation based on personal growth and successful systems. All the work and investment have truly paid off.

The Growth

I have created multiple opportunities to collaborate with like-minded people and became the best coach and speaker that I can ever be. I have enough confidence to go out and create a successful and sustaining business model. I have healed myself from the trauma that prevented me from seeing my own strengths. I have learned to listen to what my mind, body, and soul is telling me every single day, making sure that everything I do for my clients, business, and myself are in alignment with my soul. I am a heart-centered leader and truly appreciate my clients' transformation from lack of confidence and low self-esteem to owning their truest potential and living their life with full confidence and worthiness.

The Reward

My reward is being able to go on vacations with my family, having the flexibility to create a dream schedule where I can be home for my family, and understand what happiness truly feels like living a life filled with purpose and passion every single day. I am now able to step into my own confidence and let go of all the fears and judgments that were holding me back from achieving the life that I truly love and appreciate.

Prior to working with me, my client was really insecure. She did not know how to express herself and was having a hard time speaking up. She loves her family and would stay in her room and hardly communicate with her parents. She was a very quiet and private person. After working with me, she fully expresses herself, performs better in college, and creates opportunities to connect with her loved ones. She is confident about who she is becoming. She has become a great networker as a result of our work. I am looking forward to many more opportunities where I can support teenagers to be able to live their best life and rise to their true potential without feeling inadequate or insecure about who they are and who they are becoming. The teenagers are our future, and I truly believe that creating a healthier and positive mindset can solve many insecurities.

It all starts with being open to seeing what is truly possible.

The Brightness of the Future

I am now scaling my business to produce a six-figure income. I am working with over 50 teenagers, helping them increase their confidence and motivation. I have created several programs for parents and their teenagers to help close the communication gap and build a healthier relationship with one another. I am an international speaker and author, speaking in countries all around the world, inspiring teenagers to live their truest and best lives possible. I am looking forward to finding a life partner, being able to travel the world, one country at a time, and creating memories every single day to last a lifetime with my family and friends.

The Wisdom

Knowing what I know now about the secrets to my success, I offer these points:

1. Failure does not mean you are unsuccessful.

2. It is okay to be different; being unique is a beautiful gift.

3. Look for opportunities around you; they are always there.

4. Learn to say "Yes!" to the things that you are not aware of.

5. Always believe in yourself. No one is going to believe in you more than the belief you have in yourself.

6. Always listen and trust your gut; it is always right.

"Life is all about balancing being identical and different, own your truth and identity no matter what!"
~Michelle Mehta

Blessings and Love,

Michelle Mehta

Power Summary

Let's do a quick recap so that you can grasp the key concepts:

- What is it like to be unique and not like anyone else?
- Who is on your team bringing out your greatest gifts?
- What actions will you take to stay true to yourself?

Success Actions

Here are three success actions that you can take right now to make things happen in your life:

1. Create affirmations to help you increase your confidence. These are sentences that begin with "I am..." An example is "I am confident.

2. Always be in a state of gratitude. Be grateful for everything you have in your life – personally and professionally.

3. Practice meditation, sitting in silence. Breathing is your best friend.

About the Author

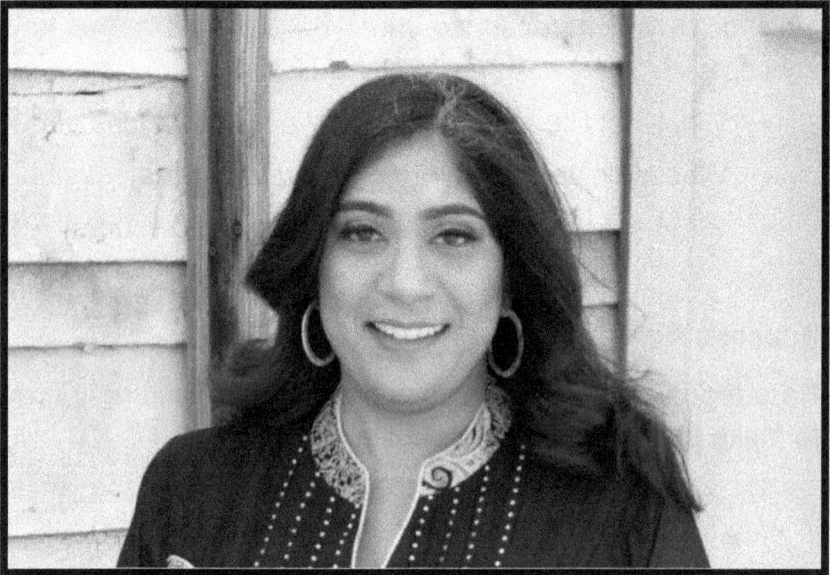

Michelle Mehta is a Certified Professional Co-Active Coach, Associate Certified Coach, and a Neuro-Linguistic Programming Practitioner.

She started her life coaching career in 2015 when she took her first class at the Co-Active Training Institute. She helps her clients find their truest version of themselves by feeling empowered and letting go of their limiting beliefs around love, worthiness, and belonging. At the end of their coaching journey, the clients are able to increase their confidence in all areas of their lives by feeling empowered, loved, and worthy. She is a Teen Confidence Coach, Mentor, and Speaker working with parents and their teenagers. She is an international coach working with clients in the US, Canada, Nigeria, and India.

She lives with her family in Irvine, California.

Business Name: Michelle Mehta Coaching

Website: www.michellemehta.com

Email: michelle@michellemehta.com

Facebook:

- **Personal:**
  https://www.facebook.com/mehta.michelle
- **Group:**
  https://www.facebook.com/groups/Teenempowerment/

Instagram: https://www.instagram.com/iammichellemehta/

LinkedIn: https://www.linkedin.com/in/michellemehta/

Products/Services:
- Teen Confidence Coaching Programs for three and six months
- Teen Confidence Group Coaching Programs for three and six months
- Speaking Engagements

Ideal Clients: Parents and their teenagers in middle and high schools.

Indomitable Spirit

Nuala K. Taylor
Transformation Coach and Reiki Master, U.S.A.

*"It amazes me every day that people will walk
around and live with a mindset that they
never created for themselves, then turn
around and try to convince others of the truth
of it when they never developed that truth
within themselves. If they are still unhappy, it
is because it was never their truth."*

~ Nuala K. Taylor

My Unforgettable Day

It began with a siren.

I am sitting in a smoking area, next to a large generator under the canopy of a makeshift, tin roof cover. The hot sun touches everything, and in August, the shade does little to stop the radiating heat that makes 102 degrees feel like 120 in Iraq. It is the 15th, but it's just another day of the very long 15-month deployment to Taji Airfield. As I took a much-needed break with a comrade, I was only two drags into a cigarette when the "Big Voice" began to wail.

That was the affectionate name that we gave to a new

early detection system for incoming attacks to our Forward Operating Base. It was 10 months into our deployment, and the first time we had a warning system. It just so happened that very day, on August 15th, that it was finally operational and online. You can probably imagine the reaction.

I'd like to say that I was completely cool-headed and acted as my training had prepared me, but I was terrified as my friend and I ran to get inside our work building, which was the closest cover from attack. All I could think was, "*Get undercover! Move, move, move! Hurry!*" while grabbing the arm of my friend and pulling him along with me.

Just when we had made it through the door, the shockwave of a missile that impacted right outside the fence line behind our office blasted my friend into my back as I collided with the pillar directly in front of me. I have no idea how long I lost consciousness, maybe for a few seconds or a few minutes, but when I was able to, I crawled under the service desk and covered my head. I was a tight ball of fear, praying that my office would not suffer a direct hit, listening helplessly while mortar after mortar, and missile after missile, created explosions, and shook the very ground that I sat upon. I could hear the radios going crazy with chatter through a high-pitched whine that took over my hearing.

It seemed like forever. Time stretched out my terror as I prayed that all of us would make it through this time. Finally, when the explosions stopped, my fear for myself was superseded by my fear for my friend and soldier who was at an unprotected guard point. So, before the "All Clear" was called, I threw on my plated battle gear, grabbed my weapon, and ran to his location, getting yelled at the whole time that it wasn't yet safe.

That day I lost so much. I lost a friend. I lost my trust in people. I lost myself. That deployment, I lost my purpose.

We lost so many comrades, so many pilots, good people who were fathers, mothers, sisters, brothers, someone's child, someone's wife or husband. In the span of one 15-month deployment, I saw the evils that people do to each other and later learned that all of it was for nothing.

I lost my faith.

Conflict

When I finally got back home, I felt an amazing relief.

I'm home!

A large weight had been lifted off me, but there was something still there, something just not right. I began wanting to work late. I did not want to go home. I yelled at my children and got into arguments with my husband for the smallest things. I terrorized them. I was always upset and tight like someone had wound me up. Sudden loud noises would make me jump or react inappropriately. I couldn't sleep, and when I did, I was having horrifying nightmares. I couldn't stay asleep. I would drink to help me sleep. I would hear and feel field artillery shake my house from ranges on the nearby Military post, hear helicopters flying over my home and roll off my bed to take cover. Conflicts at work were beginning to happen. So, I sought help.

Help came in the form of medications, 18 of them by 2014.

I developed side effects like high blood pressure, high cholesterol, tardive dyskinesia, sleep apnea, tinnitus, and each medication caused depletion of other nutrients and minerals my body needed for health in other systems. I had an undiagnosed neck injury and underwent three surgeries, but I still had pain. My mental and emotional state would swing from incredibly high states of mania only to crash into severe depression. I avoided people because I would experience anxiety from improperly identifying a person or situation as a threat which would cause my adrenaline to spike with the most violence thoughts, but because I refused to hurt anyone, I would go into fight or flight mode and suffer an anxiety attack where I would develop tunnel vision, muffled hearing, and weak legs because all the blood was rushing to my arms. I was unable to control the thoughts in my mind that would convince me of the saddest lies about myself and my life, or horrible thoughts that didn't seem like mine at all – all the while juggling a military career and trying to care for my family and my health.

The straw that broke the camel's back was when my youngest son brought home his A/B Honor Roll certificate.

My youngest is on the spectrum, and while I was dealing with what was affecting me, I also struggled to get him the services and nutrition and people that he needed to succeed. He struggled with school and cruel children and a school system that wasn't made to educate children on his level of understanding. He struggled with learning and grades for so long, that when he came home actually on the honor roll, I should have felt so happy! I should have felt so proud, like how I feel right now. However, when I told him, "*Good job, Buddy!*" I couldn't feel it. I was apathetic.

I have to be honest that I was confused at first. Why couldn't I feel proud? Then I asked myself, "*Why can't I feel happy?*" Quickly, I realized that I honestly didn't care. I couldn't feel the good feelings, and I couldn't relate emotionally to another human being, not even my son, who I love more than my life. Medications had made it easy to wake up, eat, work, rest, and get back to work, but that was it. I had learned to go numb in Iraq to protect myself and do what needed doing and instead of allowing me to feel good again, I became a psychopath. I quickly ran through some recent memories of times when I was asked anything like, *"What do you want to eat?" "Do you want to see a movie?" "Is it okay if we get chicken instead of fish today?"* And I realized that every single time, I answered with, *"I don't care."* Why? Because I didn't. I couldn't connect with myself.

I took a long look in the mirror and realized that I had allowed other people to fit me in a box that did not meet the truth of who I was and what I had accomplished. The medications were preventing me from feeling, which is integral in processing trauma. I allowed others to write my story:

> *"You are crazy, and you'll always be crazy.*
> *You aren't trustworthy enough to hold a weapon.*
> *You aren't a good Leader because you can't ignore your trauma.*
> *You can't make it without medications.*
> *You aren't good for any jobs now.*
> *No one will listen to you.*
> *You are a horrible wife and mother.*
> *It's your fault that your friend got killed.*
> *You are broken."*

My Breakthrough Moment

I spent my life being a finder of solutions, and when I realized that all these professionals were keeping me in a perpetual loop that gave me no positive results, I started thinking about Albert Einstein. I love science and theory, and he once said:

"The definition of insanity is <u>doing the same thing</u> over and over again but expecting different results."
~ Albert Einstein

If people were telling me I was not sane and put me on medications and therapies that hadn't worked for years, but doing exactly what Einstein defined as "insanity," then I reasoned that I would have to do something different regardless of what was "recommended."

I was stuck between a rock and a hard place. My life was on the line, and I needed to get a handle on my mind and my emotions and learn to overcome. My greatest fear was not losing my battle against myself. I had already experienced a lifetime's worth; it was losing the battle and leaving my loved ones behind that I loved and cared for and not being able to complete a life mission I knew I must have.

So, I stopped all my medications cold turkey.

Now, in my coaching and consulting in the holistic approach to health and wellness, I will never suggest that anyone do what I did. I will never diagnose or tell someone to stop taking medications the way I did. I always recommend that changes be made under the supervision of their physician so that when the changes that you make in your life improve your health to the point where you can reduce your medication amounts or not need them at all, the physician can see it through labs and diagnostics.

But I was desperate, and I've always been a "jump in

with both feet" kind of person. Stopping medications suddenly, and especially when your body uses them as a replacement for normal processes, can be dangerous. I was very fortunate to have been studying natural superfood detoxes in order to smooth out the process, but it was still a very trying time. During this time, I dove headfirst into every certification, years of research, and study on how to promote overall health. This journey to heal myself has brought me here to share this story with you.

My Life: Obstacles Build Strength

In my life, I have had to develop a spirit of strength and resiliency, not just for myself but also for others. I was born and grew up in Hawaii. My parents separated when I was six, which lead to divorce, but the separation left me with my mother, my four-year-old sister, and my newborn brother. We had no money, no place to live, and mom had no job skills or experience. I would learn later as an adult the dynamics of it all, but as a child, I only knew we were abandoned.

Life for us was hard, food scarce, where we lived was unstable, causing us to bounce from place to place. It was very difficult for all of us. Mom had done what she could for us to survive for 5 years but when she started dating, things got even more difficult for my siblings and me. We ended up going to my father when I was 15, who lived in another state.

Moving forward in time, I got pregnant in high school, had a run-in with some violence, was homeless for a time, and ended up moving back to Hawaii. I had my daughter my senior year of high school and walked for my diploma four weeks later. My newborn daughter and I were in danger from my mother's violent and narcissistic husband, who assaulted both us. So, with no job and no place to go, we left to be on our own.

I met my amazing husband who was also a single parent, and we developed a family. Seven years after struggling to support my family in Hawaii's economy, I joined the U.S. Army in 2001, just in time for our country to declare war after the events of September 11th. If you've ever watched any movies with basic training, you know that you either learn the game and thrive, or you don't make the cut.

So, you see, before my harrowing experience in Iraq, life had already been testing me and preparing me. I am very grateful for those hardships. Your obstacles create strength. Every hardship you have experienced brings you the opportunity to grow. You should cherish your suffering as much as you cherish what you enjoy. They are why you are still here.

Lessons Learned: Everyone You Meet is a Teacher

I was never alone during my journey, and if you've experienced hardships, trials, traumas, and painful situations – or are going through one right now – you are not alone either. There are always people who will lift you up, give you hope, shine a beacon for you, share inspiration, or kick you in the behind to get you going. I have learned from every person I have ever encountered, whether they helped me or hurt me.

I have met the most amazing human beings, normal stay-at-home moms, retired police, yoga instructors, engineers, famous media personalities, very influential and successful people that helped me turn my personal transformation into a mission. This change is due to those amazing people, but also to great business coaches I have had in my life, one very amazing therapist, and my beautiful family. Every single person in my life has helped me to strengthen my resiliency, support me, or test my resolve.

They are why I named my business "Transform YUR Life: You Under Reconstruction."

I became a Reiki master to learn to create harmony and balance in myself, others, and the world around me. My sessions and lessons help people learn about the energetic body and how quantum physics supports the ancient knowledge and practice of Reiki energy work. I work with my clients to release energies that no longer serve them, initiate breakthroughs in life, and promote stress relief.

I work with Purium Organic Superfoods to improve the world's access to foods that are clean, sustainably farmed, support organic farmers, educate people on real nutrition for real results, and aim to change the world's food supply. In this way, I can create an impact in my community.

I teach Essential Oils classes weekly on the safety and proper use of essential oils as well as how they can promote overall health by supporting the systems of the body, D-I-Y projects, and how to reduce the toxic load in the home and on your body.

I am a Transformation Coach that takes all those skills and products, and through Life Coaching, Law of Attraction principles, and relationship guidance, can help you transform any aspect of your life and teach you to be the arbiter of your life, empowering you with the tools to soar on your own. I am developing several courses to help you to become the best version of yourself. My ultimate goal is always for you to thrive past the need for my assistance.

I also help people on a digital platform that works with the power of a marketing plan for only $10 a month. This is so helpful for beginning entrepreneurs with a very small or non-existent marketing budget. It's all about branding who you are and what your passion is. You'll be able to see how you can test it out for free.

Learning Points

I want to share with you exactly how I got my physical, mental, emotional, social, and spiritual health back, and how you can tweak it to fit your individual needs. All of these learning points start with understanding the power of the statement, "I AM," and understanding that in every step of every process, you always have a choice. Your freedom to choose is why you are and always will be powerful.

Here are six secrets I use along with the Affirmations that power them.

1. Understand that you are not your trauma. What you experienced has been experienced by millions of other people over thousands of years. We choose how we see ourselves and who we become after it. We choose how we deal with that trauma.

   "I AM not a sequence of events. I choose my present and my future. I am present in the here and now. I AM happy. I AM worthy. I AM love. I AM no longer tethered by the past."

2. Conditioning the body while you learn new skills and begin to create a better version of yourself will solidify your understanding. Movement is a key to happiness. The less you move, the less you change. If you stop changing, you will become stagnant and regress in many aspects of your life.

   "I AM thankful and grateful for my body. I know that success in my health is just as important as success in life. I AM preparing my vessel for greatness."

3. Being mindful of your thoughts is key to keeping a mindset of success, happiness, abundance, and worthiness. Journaling will record your journey in times of inspiration and passion, and, in times of hardship, it will be a place to work out your thoughts and go back and remind yourself that all things ebb and flow. I have a gratitude journal, a thought journal and a dreams journal. You must respect and honor your journey; journaling can help you do this. My thought journal allowed me to analyze my thoughts and determine if my thought was really true or just a false construct of my brain. This has been an extremely powerful tool in times of depression and saved my life several times.

    "I AM capable of choosing my mindset. I AM worthy of abundance, happiness, and all I desire in this lifetime. I AM capable of seeing my obstacles as blessings."

4. Controlling your emotions can be difficult, especially when we grew up with people constantly saying, *"I can't control how I feel about that."* When in actuality, you can, and essential oils can help you do that. The part of the brain called the "amygdala" regulates your emotions, and it just so happens that your nose carries plant compounds that we recognize as "scents" to the amygdala and influences emotion. You can feel happier, energized, balanced, grounded, relaxed, peaceful, etc., and Certified Pure Therapeutic Grade oils are the safest.

    "I AM in control of how I feel at all times. I AM aware that I can choose to respond and not react. I choose to feel happiness, joy, and peace."

5. Important to the road to any recovery, is building strong and genuine relationships with others but especially yourself. This, for me, was the hardest skill to develop, because I had to learn to trust myself and my capabilities. In learning how to develop real, genuine, and true relationships with other people, I learned that there are good, honest, caring, and impact-creating humans everywhere. When I found the people who were positive, uplifting, supporting, and kept me accountable because they care about me and what I want to accomplish, I was around people that helped me to become greater. Find your soul tribe!

    "I AM a beacon of success and positivity. I will attract people who flow with me, encourage me, and keep me accountable. I AM like the 10 people I am around the most, and I choose only those that will be positive forces in my life."

6. Lastly and most importantly, I want to share a Law of Attraction pearl of wisdom that will save you time and money.

    "What you focus on expands."

    When I worked with coaches that focused on eliminating limitations and taking positive, lucrative steps, I grew. I grew so much in a short period of time because of what I focused on and whom I was working with. So, only focus on the end game, the positive mindset you need, and the steps to get there.

    "What you focus on expands."

    Who wants more of what they don't want?

"I AM focused on the goal, the benefits it will bring, and the emotion that having it and meeting it generates. I will keep the emotion of how it feels to have it, and live my day as if I already have it. I will only focus on the having."

Upwards and Uncomfortable?

I have been learning from several coaches in business, personal development, and spiritual development in my journey, and they all say the same thing. So, I'm going to pass down some wisdom to you from a person very special to me, and I hope you can share it with someone else.

Uncomfortable Is Okay; Pain Is Not

Master Sri Akarshana always tells me being uncomfortable is okay; you grow in being uncomfortable. Being uncomfortable and striving for perfection is how you achieve mastery. Pain is not okay as in pushing your limitations too far, but there is no danger in being uncomfortable, your brain is just convincing you to be afraid of something that is not real.

So, I decided to do the most uncomfortable thing – now have a *YouTube* channel where I share my story, what I have learned, and I'm allowing myself to be vulnerable and real. I'd love for you to come into a space that is positivity, love, natural solutions, and guidance.

If you are interested in Transformational Coaching or any of the developing programs in Natural Emotion Regulation, you'll love this channel.

The Reward

When I think about where I am now and what I'm able to do, I am so full of gratitude! I can choose my own hours, dedicate my time to my family when I need to, take time to do my self-care when I need to, travel, do the things that bring me happiness and help others consistently which brings me great joy.

The best part is that I'm just getting started. I finally know who I am, and there are great things on the horizon. It is my desire to see everyone at the finish line, all of you out there looking for your truth, being in the present and manifesting amazing lives!

Embrace the suck and develop a strong spirit, find your truth, and come out of it a <u>diamond</u>!

As Richard Branson says,

"Say YES! ...then learn how to do it later."

I wish for you love and light,

Power Summary

Let's do a quick check on learning to help you retain what you learned:

1. Where was I when I experienced my life-changing event?

2. What happened to me as a child that forced me to develop resiliency?

3. What three things can you keep to analyze your thoughts and record your journey?

4. What tool can help you to regulate your emotions naturally?

Success Actions

Here are Success Actions you can implement now to help you build resiliency:

- Learn to quiet the mind. Meditation is something that the most successful, influential, and powerful people do every day. Whether it is five minutes, 15 minutes, or an hour, learning to quiet the mind will help you to think with clarity.

- What situation in the past that was painful can you say taught you an important lesson?

- You must determine always to be victorious and never give up. This does not mean you will never fail. In our failings, we grow and gain strength. This means to continue to do, continue to perfect, continue to strive in all things in your life. As long as you are exerting effort to succeed, you are being victorious, and you will win!

About the Author

Nuala K. Taylor was born and raised in Hawaii and is a Native Hawaiian of mixed ancestry, directly related to King Kamehameha II, Liho Liho through the Keanaaina and Punihaole bloodlines. She is a wife of 23 years to Christopher Taylor, mother to three children, and grandmother of two. She served proudly in the U.S. Army from 2001 to 2014 retiring due to combat-related injuries. Her passion is providing services and products that improve quality of life, provide a freedom lifestyle, encourage absolute happiness, and raise the vibration of the planet.

Business Name: Transform YUR Life: You Under
Reconstruction

FREE 30 Day Trial for $10 Marketing Platform:
www.tryncp4free.site

Email: tylhealthwarrior@gmail.com

Facebook: www.facebook.com/transformyurlife

YouTube **Channel**: http://bit.ly/2QvUTYN

Products and Services:
- Purium Organic Superfoods
- Doterra
- Reiki
- Meditation
- Transformation Coach

Ideal Clients:
- People looking for balance, harmony, and stability in the body through natural solutions;
- People who need assistance with meditation, manifesting and spiritual guidance;
- People who desire to develop life skills, learning responsibility, accountability, communication, relations, societal interactions for business and personal life.

The Power of Resilience

Using Courage to Develop Your Resilience Muscle

Pix Jonasson
Resilience Coach, Australia

'Dreams with action defy logic.'
~ Pix Jonasson

The Unthinkable

If I told you that I survived not one, not two, but <u>three</u> life-threatening car accidents, would you believe me?

The first one was in November 1977, when I was seven. My mum, her mum (my gran), and I were travelling back home to Ballarat in Victoria, Australia from my cousin's First Communion several hours away. My mum was driving, and we hit a truck. My gran was killed instantly, while both mum and I were seriously injured.

The second one was in September 1992, when I was 26. My then fiancé was driving in north-west regional Victoria. You guessed it. We hit a truck! He wasn't expected to live due to his life-threatening injuries, and I was again seriously injured.

The third (and hopefully final!) life-threatening car

accident was in November 1992, only 10 weeks to the day after accident number two, and my fiancé was still in hospital! Due to exhaustion, I had a microsleep at the wheel, crashing into a mature gum tree, rolling the car, falling down an embankment with the car landing on the roof with me hanging upside down. I had to kick my way through the driver's side window, crawl out of the car, and climb up the embankment to reach to the road to call out for help. Remember, this was before mobile phones!

But I did not think, *'Why did this happen to me?'*

Rather, I actually thought, *'Why did I survive this one too?'*

I guess you could say that it was an 'Aha!' moment.

It was at that moment, standing roadside on a rural highway, that I realised I was put on this planet not to be average but to make a positive difference, not just locally, regionally, or nationally, but internationally!

This was all after I had been a victim of child sexual abuse[6] for several years by an evil, predatory neighbour, falling down a cellar, surviving an earthquake, and a few other 'learning experiences' along the way.

The Conflict

As an adult, I have always wanted to be, do, and have more in my life, but – I didn't think I was worth it.

My self-esteem was low due to the child sexual abuse I

---

[6] I must add that my beautiful parents knew <u>absolutely nothing</u> of the abuse to both myself and my sister. The minute it was disclosed, they took immediate action and it ceased. I had to make police reports and relive what had happened to me.

endured for years. I didn't think I deserved to be, do and have more.

As an adult, wife, mother, daughter, sister, aunty, employee and friend, I had also lost hundreds of thousands of dollars, faced bankruptcy, been diagnosed with depression, gone through a divorce, nursed both my dying dad and mum (who passed away in my arms in 2017) and suffered the suicide of my nephew to name a few more life lessons.

The Breakthrough and Lessons Learned

My beloved, late dad drummed communication into us as kids growing up. I was the youngest of three, now I'm the younger of two, as my sister passed away in 2018 due to alcoholism.

So, working on my own self-belief and personal development, I started to slowly believe 'I am worth it!'

One result of all my adversities is that I have developed my 'Resilience Muscle', so I want to share with you my tips so that you too can have 'The Courage to be Resilient' by using **COURAGE** to develop your own 'Resilience Muscle'.

I was born Courageous. It's in my name and my nature!

I was born in 1966 weighing only 2lbs. 2 oz, less than 1 kg, to a loving couple, Brian and Diane Cumming. So, my maiden name was Cumming. The Cumming family motto is Courage, and my late, beloved dad worked for Courage Breweries!

But this isn't about me. It's about you.

It's about 'The Power of Resilience: Using Courage to

Develop Your Resilience Muscle.'

So, what is Courage?

Courage is the ability to do something that frightens you. It's bravery. It's strength in the face of pain or grief. Other synonyms are 'pluckiness,' 'valour,' 'fearlessness,' 'intrepidness', 'nerve', 'daring', 'audacity', 'boldness', and 'gallant'. To me, it's 'backbone', 'spine', 'spirit', 'determination', 'fortitude', 'resolve', 'resolution', 'guts', 'grit', even 'spunk'. And 'Resilience' has really been on my radar and on the radar of many of my friends and colleagues, as it probably is yours!

So. what is 'Resilience'?

Resilience is the capacity to recover from difficulties or adversities – toughness.

It's the ability of a person to spring back into shape. Or, as I once heard car accident survivor Sam Cawthorn say, *'It's that bounce forward ability'*.

To me, resilience is perseverance, tenacity, dedication, all-round doggedness, staying the course.

It's your 'personal elasticity'.

So, how do you have the courage to be resilient?

I like to keep things simple, so I have created an acronym for COURAGE.

C   Connect and Communicate

O   Open Heart and Open Mind

U   Uniquely U

R   Real Relationships

A   Amazing Attitude

G   Grateful and Growing

E   Enjoy Life and Energy

C – Connect and Communicate

Reach out to people; chat with them; ask for help. It helps you be resilient. And, as they say: *'No person is an island.'*

> *'Communication - the human connection –*
> *is the key to personal and career success.'*
> ~ Paul J Meyer

O – Open Heart and Open Mind

I encourage you to have an open heart and open mind when being resilient.

Be open to needing help sometimes. Stop comparing your lowlight reel with someone's highlight reel! If you are struggling, as we all do at times, check out the abundance of tools, online and offline resources available to you.

*'Let your heart be as big as it can possibly
be.'*
~ Swami Chetanananda

And I would like to add, *'Let your heart and mind be as
big as they can possibly be.'*

U – Uniquely U

Be yourself. Be the best version of <u>you</u>.

No one else is <u>you</u>. There is only one <u>you</u> out of 7.2 billion people on this planet. <u>You</u> are special. <u>You</u> are unique. <u>You</u> matter. Fact!

*'Today you are You, that is truer than true.
There is no one alive who is
Youer than You.'*
~ Dr Seuss

R– Real Relationships

Develop real relationships with people. Really listen and be genuinely interested <u>in</u> people, not interesting <u>to</u> people.

People don't care how much you know until they know how much you care. We have two ears and one mouth. Use them in that order. A true relationship is two unperfect people refusing to give up on each other.

*'A great relationship has great
communication. That means how to
effectively express yourself and how to
listen properly.'*
~ Stephan Speaks

A – Awesome Attitude

Often people comment on my positive attitude.

Am I always so positive? Heck no! Sometimes I know I have to change my state to change my mindset. Motion creates emotion, so get into action to change your attitude.

> *'Your attitude, not your aptitude, determines*
> *your altitude.'*
> ~ Zig Ziglar

G – Grateful and Growing

Every night I write down five things I am grateful for. More recently, I now write down five things I am grateful for in the morning.

It sets my intention for the day and closes my day with a grateful heart. I am also growing my mind and body daily. I read, listen to audios, associate with positive people, and exercise!

> *'It's not joy that makes us grateful; it's*
> *gratitude that makes us joyful.'*
> ~ Unknown

E – Enjoy Life and Energy

I am very active on social media, and I often close out with *'Live Life, Love Life, Be Your Best.'*

We are only given one life, so make the most of it. Enjoy what you do. Be present.

And as for my energy, it would be remiss of me not to mention my health and wellness business.

I am fuelled by Arbonne. I love my protein smoothies in

the morning or at lunch, #vanilla or #chocolate, and I am kinda obsessed with my Fizz! Hot or Cold #citrus or #pomegranate.

The Ordinary World

For those who don't know me, my name is Pix Jonasson, and, briefly, I am a single mum of two gorgeous young adults, Sam and Katie. I am blessed to live on the beautiful Northern Beaches in Sydney, NSW, Australia.

I am the author of an upcoming book, *Think and Get Rich After Hours*.

I am also the owner of my own global social marketing business where I mentor and train entrepreneurial-minded people to create additional income by leveraging their time around their existing commitments and coach people towards Healthy Living Inside and Out.

The Drama

Facing an impending divorce, financial ruin, aka bankruptcy, feeling under-valued in my long-term career and missing my family greatly, I knew something had to change. I took charge of things and made those tough yet necessary decisions. I did this with grace and elegance in extremely trying times and I have come through it all thanks to my Courage and Resilience.

I am not a victim. I am a <u>victor</u> and I love that I get the honour and privilege to help others be victors too.

The Call to Action

With my 'learning experiences', adversities, challenges, and all my personal development, I have Courage and Resilience in bucketloads.

I aim to understand people's problems, pains, and challenges before proposing solutions. Being an entrepreneur takes resilience. I have done it, and I started my own online business. I use social media to help entrepreneurs, coaches, consultants, business owners, and employees design and live their best life.

Reach out to me if you would like to be mentored, or if you want further information on my health and wellness business or our '30 Days to Healthy Living Program'.

If you're serious about living your best life, schedule a free 45-minute strategy session with me here:

pix@pixjonasson.com

The Growth and Brightness of the Future

Since being a government employee, I knew I wanted to be, do and have more. Not only that, I wanted to give more.

I have used The Power of Resilience to develop two respective businesses.

- My communications business: Coaching/Speaking;
- My health and wellness business: a global online, botanically based health and wellness business operating in Australia, Canada, New Zealand, Poland, U.K., and U.S.A.

www.pixjonasson.arbonne.com

My Coaching/Speaking program includes:
- ✓ **The Pix Factor:** One-on-one, private, personalised coaching;

✓ **Dynamic Mastermind Group:** Private peer support group coaching;

✓ **Keynote Presentations/MC**

If you want to find out more about my work, just email:

pix@pixjonasson.com

...and we'll have a chat or connect with me on:

Facebook: https://www.facebook.com/pix.jonasson

...or

LinkedIn: https://www.linkedin.com/in/thepixjonasson/

...or

Instagram: pixjonasson

...or

Skype: pix2166

The Reward

I am so happy and thankful that I have the grit, determination and Resilience to run a successful business online, connecting with people globally and making an international impact.

With both my online business and my coaching/speaking, I am blessed to changes lives, spiritually, emotionally, mentally, physically, socially, environmentally, and financially.

I can take operate my business anywhere in the world as long as there is Wi-Fi! I love that I am a geographic, digital entrepreneur, and that I can help others achieve the same.

The Wisdom

So, with all the times in my life that I have personally had to be resilient, including losing my 31-year-old nephew to suicide a couple of years ago, here's my personal strategy for The Power of Resilience: Using **COURAGE** to develop your resilience muscle….

C	Connect and Communicate
O	Open Heart and Open Mind
U	Uniquely U
R	Real Relationships
A	Amazing Attitude
G	Grateful and Growing
E	Enjoy Life and Energy

And always remember that:
- You can have the power of Resilience by using **COURAGE**;
- You are amazing; and
- You matter!

Thank you for sharing your precious time with me. I truly appreciate that and am grateful.

Have an awesome morning, afternoon, or evening wherever in this magnificent world you are.

Quote

> '*We can't take charge of everything in our*
> *lives, but we can take charge of our*
> *thoughts. Take charge of them wisely!*'
> ~ Pix Jonasson

Live Life, Love Life, Be Your Best!

Dream Big!

P. Jonasson

Pix Jonasson

Power Summary

Let's do a quick recap so that you can grasp the key concepts of resilience and being resilient. Here's my personal strategy for The Power of Resilience: Using **COURAGE** to Develop Your Resilience Muscle:

C	Connect and Communicate
O	Open Heart and Open Mind
U	Uniquely U
R	Real Relationships
A	Amazing Attitude
G	Grateful and Growing
E	Enjoy Life and Energy

Success Actions

Here are three success actions that you can take right now to make you more resilient, personally and professionally:

1. Actively engage in personal and professional development. Contact me at pix@pixjonasson.com to discuss this further.
2. Write down one thing that you need to focus on and improve to be more resilient in your life and business?
3. Remember one time when you felt resilient, strong, courageous. Write it down.

About the Author

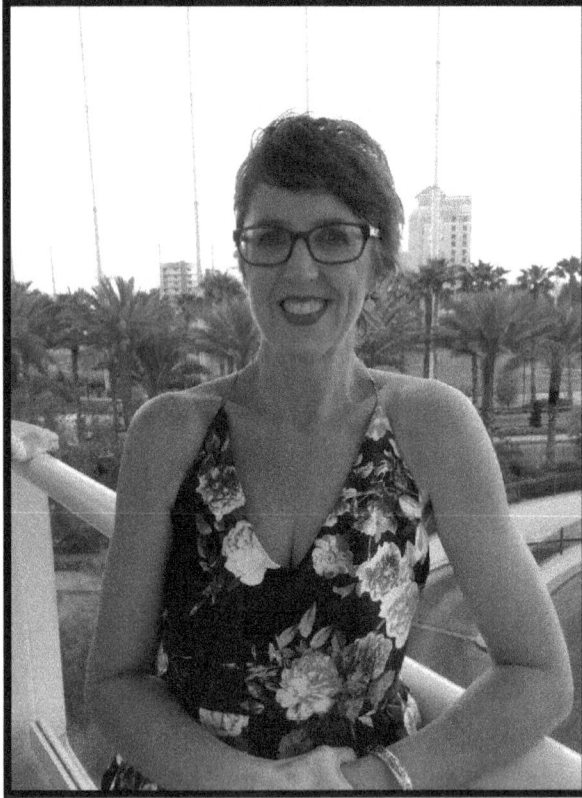

Pix Jonasson is an author, speaker, dynamic funpreneur, courageous connector, passionate health & wellness advocate, edu-tainment pro and lifestyle coach. She is also a happiness agent, an international public speaker and mental performance coach. Her mission is to positively impact people – one person at a time.

Pix is also the owner of her own health and wellness business, successfully developing a global social marketing empire in all six countries of operation. She is also successfully growing her educational, motivational, training, and consulting business dedicated to helping individuals and businesses alike explode their personal or professional success.

Pix's new book, *Think and Get Rich After Hours* showcases seven leading 'success creation' experts. It is written for those who know that they have what it takes but keep falling short, and for those who may already be wildly successful but want to take their personal and professional lives to the next level.

Pix has developed the M.E.N.T.O.R.S. Method of Success© and is committed to providing excellent courses, events, information, coaching and training to people to enable them to achieve their success.

Proven Track Record

Ever-courageous Pix is not new to overcoming adversity, connecting with people, or making things happen. She is recognized as a 'linchpin', the woman who brings people together to achieve the desired outcomes for issues of local, regional, national, and international significance. She provides the solutions to her clients' and audience's needs. Pix has over 30 years experience in marketing, communications, event management and public speaking, working in both the public service field and private enterprise. She is instrumental in liaising with local, state and federal businesses and government agencies, media, landholders, stakeholders, clients and the general public.

She has been awarded the following:

- 2019 Global Goodwill Ambassador
- 2010 Internet Best Practice Awards - Best Youth Initiative Award Finalist

Business Name: Pix Jonasson

Website: www.pixjonasson.arbonne.com
(Health and Wellness)

Email: pix@pixjonasson.com

Facebook: https://www.facebook.com/pix.jonasson

Instagram: https://www.instagram.com/pixjonasson/

LinkedIn: https://www.linkedin.com/in/thepixjonasson/

Ideal Clients: Pix works with people who are not where they want to be personally or professionally. Her ideal clients are driven, passionate, heart-centred, kind, caring, and loving people of integrity with a positive, can-do work ethic, who want to make a positive impact in their life and the lives of others.

Persistence, Intuition, and Adaptability

Rina Pineda Strauss
Management Consultant, USA

"Intuition will always steer you in the right direction. Listen to it. Love it. Trust it. Hone it!"

~ Rina Pineda Strauss

How Time Flies!

The other day, I was signing a client document and dated the year as 2020. It was the first time I had done so in the new year, and I was taken aback. Twenty years have flown by since I started my sales and sales management career! It's been a career fraught with challenges, joys, surprises, and never-ending changes. I've loved nearly every second of it. However, as most things worth having and fighting for in life, it was never easy. The "never easy" aspect of my career is one I am incredibly grateful for as it pushed me and challenged me always to improve and be better.

I hope it never becomes easy!

Developing A Work Ethic, or Thanks, Fun-loving College Friends!

As I look back at my 20-year career, I think about the character traits I developed or had an innate sense of that helped me succeed in a demanding role. The first that comes to mind is **Persistence** – the ability to push through even the most challenging circumstances or people. It means always knowing what was true for me and my commitment to get it done even if there were those that didn't believe in me. It was in university where my persistence started to show itself in my life and help me in moments where I would have been lost without it.

I attended one of the most expensive universities in New York. I was proud to have been accepted and overjoyed and humbled to have received enough scholarships and grants to attend the school without financial constraints. At the behest of my parents and my own interest in the subject, I pursued a degree in biology with the intent of attending medical school upon my graduation. Although I worked hard, it was disheartening to me to see how my new friends, with very little effort, achieved high marks, sometimes higher than mine, although I was studying all the time! Seeing their effortless success was hard and caused me to doubt my ability as a biology major, and I was plagued by defeatist thoughts.

- *"I guess I'm not as smart as my friends."*
- *"No matter how hard I work, I'll never be able to achieve the near-perfect grade point averages my friends achieve."*
- *"What is wrong with me that I can't skip class and cram over a weekend to do a whole semester's worth of work like my friends do and still get great grades?"*

Still, it was my persistence that pushed me through to succeeding with a challenging major. My real breakthrough happened once I stopped comparing myself to my friends. Yes, they had time for parties and dating and barely studied, but I was developing a work ethic that would serve me richly in my chosen career. Also, I loved and valued my friends and didn't want my jealousy over their academic success despite their lack of studying or classwork cause me to resent them.

Because they spend more time socializing than studying, the times we spent together was great fun! They told terrific jokes, had interesting stories, and were sparking conversationalists. I decided if I wasn't going to be as smart as them, I would work hard and enjoy them as a respite from my constant studying and research.

I'm Not Leaving – You'll Have to Force Me Out!

More challenges soon abounded in my chosen major. The school had great pride and a reputation of nearly all of their biology majors graduating in four years and being admitted to medical schools and postgraduate science careers. One way they were able to ensure this continued success was by encouraging students who were struggling to drop the program in their sophomore year. I remember vividly one of my classmates in tears after a meeting with a guidance counselor at the school who had encouraged her to remove herself from the major because she was not able to score beyond a B GPA in the program. I remember thinking no matter what my own guidance counselor told me, I would never drop my biology major.

My turn came soon enough. With a B-plus in my biology major and a perfect A in my English minor, I thought my counselor interview would be smooth sailing.

It was anything but!

I still remember the counselor's concerned look on her face discussing my continued participation in the biology program. She remarked that since I was achieving a perfect A in my minor and could never get to an A in most of my biology courses, it was time to throw in the towel and leave the biology program. She remarked how much happier I'd be switching to an English major since I had a perfect 4.0 there. Never mind that the two programs combined with the school's required liberal arts courses had resulted in a very respectful GPA that teetered between a B+ and an A-. Her final words were that I needed to heed what my grades were telling me and drop the biology major as the courses were only going to get harder, and I would fall further behind my classmates.

To this day, I still remember my reaction. She had barely finished her words when I got up quickly, pushed my chair behind me, and said unless I was forced to, I would <u>not</u> be abandoning my biology major. She was taken aback and said something to the effect that it was my decision, but it was against her recommendation. I told her I didn't care, and I would persist as a biology major.

My persistence had carried me through to continue in the major that I loved and that I felt was right for me. By my senior year, I had a 3.8 GPA, I was on the Dean's List and further convinced my persistence had pushed me in the right direction.

In that experience, I knew persistence was propelling me forward, but there was something else, and it was a trait that, as I continually honed, it has served me well in my career. That is **Intuition** – the almost uncanny ability to know when a situation was worth pursuing and when I should leave it alone. My intuition repeatedly told me a biology degree was right for me, and I obeyed that little voice. It has yet to send me on the wrong path!

So, how did a B.S. in Biology and later a Master's in Biology serve me in my eventual chosen career in sales and management? Immensely. The analytical, research, and presenting skills I honed during my biology career have helped me understand, build upon and embrace data, and present it in a confident and persuasive matter that has resulted in many client success stories throughout my career.

Wall Street and the Beach

I started on Wall Street in 2000. When I tell my clients and sales teams that in 2000 we had just begun to use emails and cell phones were merely phones used to call and leave voice messages only, they struggle to believe me! Adaptability has allowed me to embrace all the rapid changes that happened throughout my career and will continue to happen.

After a successful 10-year career on Wall Street, intuition began calling out to me again. I have always loved the beach and especially loved visiting Florida whenever I could. I loved the idea of living in beautiful, sunny weather all year round and not deal with the bitter cold of New York. I started marinating on the idea of leaving my family, career, and everything I knew and move to Florida. Never did I feel that stronger than in October 2009 when that desire grew to a boiling point. I still have the countless emails I wrote to my mentors, best friends, and family that October that I needed to get to Florida, that my intuition was pushing me there, and if I didn't heed that voice that never steered me wrong before, I would miss out on something truly special.

I moved to Florida on March 23rd, 2010. I sold my financial practice and left New York with no solid job offer in Florida or even a permanent place to stay. I told myself I would have a great job, a great home, and even a great guy to date within three days of my arrival. My friends and family who have always known me as an eternal optimist thought I was too impulsive in my decision and that it was highly unlikely I would find all three within my first three days in my new city.

Intuition told me to push as hard as I could during those three days. It guided me to conferences and networking events and business chambers where I could find all three, and I trusted its magic to come through for me. March 23rd, 2009 was a Monday. By Wednesday evening on March 25th, three days later, I had accepted a great job offer leading a 50-person sales team for one of the largest advertising firms in the state; I had found a great apartment in a desirable neighborhood; and at a business conference, met a great, very handsome guy that I dated for two months and remain *Facebook* friends with to this day.

Destiny

I still wondered what it was all about October 2009 the prior year that had called out to me so strongly to come to Florida.

Two months later, I received my answer.

On May 23rd, two months to the day I had arrived in Florida, I went to an early morning volleyball meet on the beach with some close friends. There I was introduced to the sweetest, funniest, smartest, and kindest man I ever met. His blue eyes sparkled as we talked that day, and our first meeting at the volleyball court turned into a day-long date that finally ended around 8 p.m. that night, and then only because we both had to work the next day.

That man was my future husband, and later the father to our precious child. He and our baby are my everything. He had moved to Florida in October the prior year to complete his master's degree. I laughed when he told me months later, as I finally had my answer as to why my intuition called out to me so strongly that past October when I made the life-altering decision to leave behind everything I knew to follow it, even leaving behind my beloved sister, my close-knit community, and all my dear friends. I trusted my life to intuition, and it never steered me wrong. We women have such a precious gift that our wonderful fathers, boyfriends, and husbands look on with wonder and curiosity as to why they don't have it or experience it as much as we do. That gift is intuition. Listen to it. Trust it. Hone it! It will make all your dreams come true if you let it.

Sales

Adaptability is another great trait to have as a sales expert and management consultant. The skills of sales and leadership are critical to the success of any company. From my role at the advertising firm, I transitioned to a technology company as I was fascinated with technology perhaps as a remnant interest during my years as a biology major. Advertising and technology could not be more different! However, the same sales and management skills I developed on Wall Street easily transitioned to my role at the advertising firm and later into the world of technology, on which I currently focus my sales consulting.

Although I can and do work successfully with other industries and dramatically increase their sales, it is the technology sector that many of my clients come from. One of my clients a few years ago was looking to increase their sales from $300,000 per month to $750,000 per month. When I reviewed their sales training manual and met with the sales team, I silently told myself I could easily get them to $1,000,000 per month rather quickly.

We accomplished that within three months' time simply

by creating standards for call times, call volumes, and providing feedback on every call. We've had many other similar success stories. If your company is struggling with increasing sales, email us at:

rpscorp@mail.com

   As I look back at the path I took to success as a sales consultant, I see that it had several key factors:

1. Know and trust what you value and what feels right for you despite the opinions of so-called experts. No matter what a highly regarded university guidance counselor told me, I knew I would stay in the major I felt was my calling.

2. Don't compare yourself to others. My party-loving, straight-A friends in college were gifted with the ability to score well on tests while studying very little. I had my own gifts. When I stopped comparing myself to them, I was able to appreciate them more.

3. Listen, honor, and respect your intuition; it will never steer you wrong.

4. Take action on your dream, no matter how inconvenient! I wanted to enjoy the beach and sun all year round even if it meant abandoning the life I enjoyed and leaving dear friends and family behind in New York.

5. Be a chameleon, ready to adapt to all kinds of changing business environments.

Power Summary: The Three Horsemen

Persistence, **Intuition**, and **Adaptability** have all helped hone and guide my career in so many ways. They are my "three horsemen" that always help me prepare for challenges and lead me to new levels of achievement and client success.

I promise you that if you let them guide you, despite what those around you may say or think to discourage you from heeding them, they will lead you to the best and most unexpected joy and success. They did for me, and they can for you, too! Listen to them, apply action to their message, and they will always steer you in the best possible direction and make all your dreams come true.

"Stop comparing yourself to others. We all have our own unique gifts. Find yours and develop them."
~ Rina Pineda Strauss

Success Actions

Here are four Success Actions you can do today to get closer to your goals tomorrow:

1. Develop your **Persistence** by doing something every single day for 1-5 minutes. The key is to get to at least 30 days in a row of completing an action with no excuses, come rain or shine. It can be a short exercise like journaling or learning a new language or skill. The possibilities are endless.

2. Develop and hone your **Intuition** by silencing your thoughts throughout your day and allowing intuition to guide you. Listen to it as it tells you whether to walk to the right or walk to the left, picks out your outfit for the day, and even what time it tells you to go to bed.

3. To practice and apply **Adaptability** into your life, learn a new technology you are not currently comfortable with and practice using it.

4. Create goals that excite you and create action plans to obtain them. It doesn't matter if your goals are inconvenient, very challenging to achieve, and require some sacrifice. These harder-to-reach goals are all the more satisfying when they are accomplished.

About the Author

Rina Pineda Strauss is a management consultant based in Florida.

She honed her client selling and listening skills during a successful 10-year career on Wall Street. Her passion is consulting clients on how to dramatically increase their sales. Rina firmly believes any company will struggle to grow without a well-trained and motivated sales team. She analyzes and reviews all sales data of her client companies and helps their sales teams reach KPIs previously not considered possible. She does this by breaking down large projects into smaller ones.

For example, Rina institutes a minimum 2,000-call-volume-per-month for many of the sales teams of her client companies. To achieve this, she simply encourages the sales team to make at least 30 calls per day – that is only 15 calls in the morning and 15 calls in the afternoon. At the end of the month, her sales team members are always surprised to learn how much they dramatically increased their call volume from a few hundred calls to 2,000+ calls simply by committing to making 15 calls in the morning and 15 calls in the afternoon.

To learn how Rina can help your company's sales teams dramatically increase their sales, email Rina at:

rpscorp@mail.com

LinkedIn:
https://www.linkedin.com/in/rina-pineda-strauss-5288894/

Services: Management consulting services to dramatically increase your company's sales.

Ideal clients: $400,000/year sales revenue companies looking to dramatically increase their sales, especially technology firms.

5 Ways to Unleash Your Financial Power

Ronica Brown
CPA and Entrepreneur, U.S.A.

"Every day, the clock resets. Your wins don't matter. Your failures don't matter. Don't stress on what was, fight for what could be.

~ Sean Higgins

What would it feel like to finally overcome your financial difficulties and end your money stress?

The reality is most people think having a lot more money is the only solution to their financial problems, but this is far from the truth. Several years ago, I found myself dissatisfied with the direction of my life. I had a great job, a good paycheck, and I was able to travel and experience many of the finer things in life. I was basically living the life that I thought I always wanted. However, over time climbing the corporate ladder lost its appeal and I felt trapped in the rat race. I knew I had to make a change in my life and that's when I turned to the idea of becoming an entrepreneur.

I started to research how to become successful in business.

My personality likes to rely on logic and facts, so naturally, I was hoping I would uncover a formula to follow - a study guide, a checklist or clear path to take. However, after searching for a while, I couldn't find it! Throughout my graduate and undergraduate years, I had some type of checklist to follow: I knew that after I got my Bachelor's degree, I would get a Master's, and I knew step by step what that would entail. Once I became a certified public accountant, I lost the structure I had come to know and love. Now, I wasn't quite sure what to expect from life and how to make a difference, or what to explore in order to take my life to the next level. I knew I needed to do something differently.

After working with a wide range of individuals, I encountered scenario after scenario where individuals who had wealth from their careers, a lottery win, or an inheritance soon became broke. It was then that I realized that more money doesn't always fix our money problems. What I have found is most people suffer from their money habits, regardless of their income. You can earn a lot and still be poor, and that's what many people find hard to accept.

More Money, Means Needing More Knowledge

If you listen to any of the financial education gurus, you will learn that the more money you have, the more you will have to know about your money to make the best use of it.

Starting a business was an eye-opening adventure for me and my money life. When I worked in corporate America, I had the house, the expenses, and everything a young professional thinks would make an ideal life. But I was still struggling financially with growing credit card debt and living paycheck to paycheck. Each time I got an increase or a bonus, it was already spent before it even entered my bank account. Did I mention that I was single, living in Georgia (a lower cost of living state), making over six figures but still feeling extremely poor? I needed a way to fix this money problem. I couldn't imagine living the rest of my life like this. Everyone loves a story where they become rich. Although it feels good to think about being wealthy, for many people, it seems too daunting to do the work to get closer to their financial goals. What everyone misses is the journey and sacrifice that they will have to make for this to happen. At this point, you may have read all the books, attended conferences, and have an idea of how much money you want to have in your life. But the years come and go and despite your best intentions, you're still struggling to keep the money saved and move forward with these plans.

Where do you start?

What you are experiencing is not uncommon. It may feel like a different planet because you may convince yourself that you're not a numbers person and you don't understand. If you're like most people, you may feel that the answer to your financial problem is one of the following:

- "...when I start making more money;"
- "...when I have X amount saved or invested;"
- ...and one of the most common ones, "...when I am debt-free."

Here's the truth: while all of the above are great aspirations, without a solid financial plan, having more money will only create bigger problems for you. You may find that the more you earn, the greater your expenses are. Even if you pay off past debt, you may start accumulating new debt. If you are in an unfavorable financial situation and you don't change your habits, this cycle will repeat itself year after year.

The best place to start moving towards experiencing

financial freedom is to realize this is more about <u>you</u> being in control of <u>your finances</u>, rather than <u>your finances</u> being in control of <u>you</u>. Being in control just simply means you have a plan for every penny you make.

To get to this place means you will have to decide on a long-term plan for your money.

Is it:

- Having enough to retire?
- Paying for your kids' college?
- Going on luxury vacations?
- Investing?
- Space travel?

What is it that you really want? Once you decide on your "long term plan", then you can start developing small, action steps to move forward.

In a 2017 interview with *Vanity Fair*,[7] billionaire Mark Cuban talks about making small, habit changes. A billionaire is concerned about how much cash he spends that he buys household supplies in bulk for the entire year or two when they are on sale. He recommended picking one item to do that so that you can start trying to see how you can save money.

My way was not as modest as he recommended. I went in for a big change! I decided to downsize my entire life. My long-term plan is to be an entrepreneur owning and investing in multiple businesses. I put my house up for rent and went from a three-story, four-bedroom house to what I

---

[7] http://video.vanityfair.com/watch/mark-cuban-s-guide-to-getting-rich

really needed, a one-bedroom and bathroom, with a shared living space and kitchen. This was one year before I decided to quit my job, so I had the luxury of the same paycheck but with rental revenue helping pay down my mortgage. This was a big step that enabled me to pay off my credit cards and put 50% of my paycheck into savings.

The big shift in your own money life doesn't have to be as drastic as mine. It can be achieved by implementing a few simple steps and habit changes. You can start these a month at a time so that you can plan lasting changes that are easy to implement and stay consistent.

If you're tired of not taking action, eager to make significant changes in your financial situation, then these steps will help you to make lasting changes. I hope you have discovered that just having money goals will not be enough to enable you to achieve the financial freedom you desire, because you will see the massive impact when you are able to make these changes and then meet your money goals.

The shift must be in your habits.

Track Your Spending - A big mistake is that most people make when they attempt to fix their money problems is to start off with creating a budget, but they set unrealistic budgets they're unable to stick to and feel discouraged and helpless after the first month. The first habit change is just to start tracking what you are spending before you set a budget, to get a clear view of your spending.

At the beginning of a new month, download an app, connect your bank accounts and credit card accounts, and start tracking everything. Before I decided to downsize my life, I downloaded the app *Mint* from the recommendation of a close friend. I was a stubborn CPA who wanted to keep things in Excel, which I thought was easier for me, but the real-time tracking of this app completely changed things for me. I was able to see everything in real-time! Now, I had visibility and an easy way to see all my spending patterns without spending a lot of time. I had to face what was going on in my bank account. The next month, I started to eliminate unnecessary expenses, including eating out a bit less which also helped me lose a few extra pounds that I was accumulating over late-night drinks.

Review Your Spending Patterns: It only makes sense to keep track of something if you are going to use the information. This is where the second strategy comes in. This is where you review your spending pattern. Set up an hour on your calendar every month and have a date with your money. Don't make it stressful, and this is why you don't start off with making a budget or saving money or any of these goals. What you are basically doing is observing yourself. This will help you to see what is real and what expenses you can change.

Once you are able to see where you are wasting money or where you can cut back, it is then you have started gaining your financial power. Now you can start planning. Next month, you can tackle one expense. You gain some consistency by managing that expense. Then the next month or two, you move to the next.

To be successful, you have to make habit changes slowly if you want to make lasting change. If you have an appetite for big jumps, then go for them! The key is thinking long term and knowing that you will see it through.

The key here is, make it easy for yourself so that you can be consistent and start training and building your new financial muscles. This will start the momentum for you to gain your financial power and start making decisions that will be rewarding.

Allocate Your Money: Growing up, I remembered seeing my grandmother, who was a vendor in an open market in Ocho Rios, Jamaica, allocated her money. When she returned from a weekend of selling fruits and vegetables, she had money wrapped in different pieces of plastic bags, all stored in her brasserie. One Sunday morning, I was watching her undoing these pieces of plastic. I asked her if it wouldn't be easier for her to put everything in one pile and she looked at me and smiled and continued what she was doing. Now, I understand that she was allocating her money. She was putting aside for each expense that she had, and also to restock her shelves for the upcoming weekend at the market

In its simplest form, you can do this too. This is where you start to allocate your money. This is where you have a plan for each dollar. For example, 10% or $1,000, to savings each month. You can use a percentage of your after-tax paycheck/earnings or a fixed dollar amount per month. This is when you start setting a pattern that you know will work for you. This is when budgeting will finally make sense. A budget is a blueprint of how you plan to spend your money.

Gain Some Financial Knowledge: These steps will help you to feel more in control of your money and remove the myths that you have told yourself over the years. Now is the time to start planning for bigger goals and take massive steps to financial freedom and wealth-building. This is when you start gaining some financial knowledge. This is financial literacy, where your goal is to understand how money works and what is the best way to use your money to meet your long-term goals. There are numerous conferences, books, and resources on the market that will open your mind to all the tools that are available to help you along the way.

You should also consider meeting with a few financial planners to understand how they work and how they can help you achieve your goals.

Understand Your Taxes: The other most impactful financial tool is your taxes. The best I can advise you here is to understand your taxes. This does not mean to learn how to prepare your taxes but understand the basics of taxes so you can see how much money you may be losing. This is the money the IRS doesn't even ask for, but too many Americans pay more in taxes each year because they just don't know. This is where you can also see some extra cash in your pocket.

Don't make it overwhelming; what you can do is look at your return. Just take 30 minutes after the filing is completed and look at it. Read each line item that you see a number on. This will set off some light bulbs for you. As a tax consultant, my best clients are the ones who know a bit about how taxes work. They are easier to work with because when I introduce a tax-saving strategy that will significantly reduce their taxes, they are ready for it.

You see, you may be overpaying on your taxes because your tax person doesn't know how to help you, and you don't know what questions to ask because you don't know anything about it. You can start with this one question, "Do you have any suggestions on how I can reduce my taxes?"

You see, the savvy strategies are reserved for those who are ready to receive the information.

In our day to day lives, the word "budget" carries the

sense of negativity and hardship that people become scared of the word "budget".

What? A budget? "A budget makes me feel like I will have to go back to eating Ramen noodles," one friend once said to me.

The main issue here is we have a relationship with money that has been ingrained in us from childhood and other experiences. Some people are open to talk about money freely and want to fix the problem. Most people, on the other hand, make it more top-secret than their medical record.

Mindset is Everything: Over the years, our relationship with money becomes ingrained in our subconscious mind making it harder to change. Just like you have a relationship with humans, you also have a relationship with objects and things such as money. This is where it gets into a mindset and how you really think and feel about money and the purpose of money.

For example, some people don't want to think they need to justify being focused on having good financial habits because they may have grown up where money wasn't discussed much, or the subject of money was always negative. Later in life, this may cause inaction to fix this problem due to fear of feeling incapable.

Think about your thoughts around money and why you need it in your life.

Think about spending patterns and how spending makes you feel.

We have to understand this so that when we start developing new money habits, we have to be able to recognize when the old money habits start to fight back, be prepared to resist and fight the old habits with your new habits until they become who you are.

It's a daunting experience wanting to make a change, but each year you feel that you just continue the same as usual. For others, they may lift themselves up with the dream of that bigger paycheck and those higher-revenue months. I watch this happen over and over again when the big checks do come in but get eaten up faster than it took to make it.

Businessman and author Robert Kiyosaki's book *Rich Dad and Poor Dad* outlined this particular situation between a college-educated Ph.D. dad who chose the tradition way of thinking about money which includes: go to school, get a good job, climb the ladder, prize stability over independence, buy a house, and spend money without a clear long-term plan. This is the "poor dad." The "rich dad," on the other hand, was a high-school drop-out whose view on money was to work for a salary if you have to but aim for financial independence; have your money generate more money and take calculated risks boldly.

The "poor dad" mindset is the one the most people operate in, including me at one point. I remember the big house, the big mortgage, the bills, the clothing, the trips, etc., and the rat race that keeps us increasing expenses. Then, for most of us, people get married, children come, and the cycle goes on for years until we discover that we don't have enough money to retire.

In his book, Robert Kiyosaki discussed that most people are not able to achieve the "rich dad" mindset because of five personality traits that hamper human beings: fear, cynicism, laziness, bad habits, and arrogance. The one I used to battle with is fear, and the ones the most people I come across battle with are fear and bad habits. But more profoundly, the biggest lesson in this story is the mindset and habits it will take to achieve financial independence and wealth.

But no one has given us the cheat sheet, the roadmap, or a customized solution that we can just blindly follow to fix this problem. Then life happens, as it should, and other priorities take control of our lives. The years go by, and the financial problems just stay there - like the elephant in the room. Then we start feeling helpless, telling yourselves that we are not good with money or we are not a numbers person.

Yes, we often resort to demeaning ourselves and accept things as they are.

Habit changes are the fix for a lasting solution with your money. It is not easy because you will have to look at yourself in your mirror and understand that you yourself are the solution.

This is the missing step that is keeping you in the same place that you have been for years. Yes, keep your goals of getting out of debt and making more money, but none of this will change until you start to make habit changes.

Finally, you will be able to find a customized solution for yourself and your family. You will have your own cheat sheet! Now, everything will start making sense. Your solution will be customized for you and not just be a "one size fits all" solution that never works.

Now you can start setting milestones on achieving your long-term plan for your wealth. Do you want to invest in businesses, stocks, real estate, etc.? What will be your next move that will excite you and make this even more rewarding? The future is here, and you're in control. You can see a way to finally experience financial freedom. You will see your job differently, your clients, your business, etc.

It all will start making sense.

Once I was able to start taking control of my money, I had less money coming in, but I was making the best use of the money that I already have. Within two years, I was making extremely profitable real estate deals, I have more money invested, and my CPA practice had finally started paying me and my bills. I was free! I could now see how I could completely achieve financial freedom by putting investments in place that will continue to make me money.

I still use my app to track my spending and add a new type of investment each year. Recently, I started learning more about life insurance and different products that I am able to use to help me reach my financial goals. So, you don't have to wait to be a "millionaire" to start a path to financial change. Once you start having good money habits, the rewards will start to accumulate, and you will live to see the lasting effects.

Love, Ronica

Power Summary

- Making habit changes is where you will see the big shift in your money life and will be the most rewarding moving forward.

- Don't make this a job! Make it simple, and your goal is to be consistent. Slow and steady will win this race.

- Never start with a budget.

Success Actions:

- Start tracking all your spending. Use an app to automate the process so that it's easy for you to do!

- Review your spending patterns so that you can start making small changes.

- Start to make habit changes slowly. Tackle one expense one month at a time to start building consistently.

About the Author

Ronica Brown

I am a mom to a happy, bright-eyed, 13-month-old son who is allowing me to see life from different angles and helping me enjoy the magic in the present moments. I have lived in three different countries so far and looking forward to more travels, love, and laughter with my new family.

I am a certified public accountant (CPA) and business tax expert. After completing my master's degree in accounting and taxation, I worked 11 years helping high-net-worth individuals and corporations to reduce their taxes. Now, I use these same concepts to help small businesses implement money-saving strategies that are designed to reduce their taxes and keep more money in their pocket. I am also passionate about business and social entrepreneurship and volunteer my time to teach young adults the value of entrepreneurship to build strong communities.

Business Name: Ronica Brown Agency

Website: https://ronicabrownagency.com/

Email: ronica@ronicabrownagency.com

Facebook: @ronicabrownagency

Instagram: Taxninja_ronicabrown

LinkedIn:
www.linkedin.com/in/ronicabrowncpataxandacounting

Services: Tax Reduction Planning and Tax Consulting

Ideal Clients: Business owners who normally owe $50K or more on their taxes.

I can help them reduce their tax bill and start building tax-free wealth.

Inside Out

First Step to a Successful and Joyful Life

Snehal R. Singh
Author, Business Coach, Writer's Coach,
Publisher, International Keynote Speaker,
U.S.A.

"A deep sense of love and belonging is an irreducible need of all people. We are biologically, cognitively, physically, and spiritually wired to love, to be loved, and to belong. When those needs are not met, we don't function as we were meant to. We break. We fall apart. We numb. We ache. We hurt others. We get sick".

~ Brene Brown

"What is the opposite of loneliness? Is it belonging?" I asked myself while I had a sip of warm chai on a snowy day. While I was enjoying the snow from my room window, I looked inside to find absolute silence.

Everything was calm. It was just me, and I found myself asking again, *"Am I lonely?"* or *"Am I alone?"* and something inside me said, *"You are happy"*.

Indian weddings are loved all around the world. Mine came eight years ago; it was the most beautiful time of my life. My Prince Charming was marrying me after 11 years of being in love. It took us nearly seven of those years just for his parents to say, "Yes". My Prince Charming is the most perfect man I could ever ask for. I was going to have a perfect wedding and, to be honest, it was. We had a grand wedding. All our relatives and loved ones blessed us. However, in midst of it all, if I were to have paused for a second, and asked that Snehal, *"Are you Happy? Is this what you wished for?"*

I would have said, "No". Don't get me wrong. I was on cloud nine marrying the guy of my dreams who was also my first love. However, I was not 100% happy. You know when you sense that his family doesn't like you enough. Yes, that feeling – it sucks. Pardon my French, but in any world, that doesn't sit well. You feel like an outsider all the time. You know those smiles are fake, and you feel sick to your stomach. The wedding ceremony was beautiful. The next day, the mundane caught up.

I spent every day thinking either, *"What could I do so that my in-laws would love me just as they loved my co-sister? What could I do to feel accepted?"* or, *"What is so wrong with me? Why doesn't anyone love me?"*

While these thoughts sound so cliché now, they were my everyday truth then.

So, what did I do? I came up with different ways to win everyone's hearts. I attended and organized all family meetings. I called everyone home. I cooked their favorite food. I went out of my way to just see them smile. I stretched and stretched – until I broke.

Now, you may say that's all natural. Yes, it is, but

eventually, when all these feelings started to bottle up, I changed. I changed into someone who was short-tempered, snappy, and absolutely unapproachable. I had put on weight and started hating everything around me. I was amazing at body-shaming myself. I lived with six people in a small home, crying every night.

I used to smile when my husband was in town, and every time he was on tours, I would complete all my chores. I would make sure everyone was asleep after I told them I would watch TV for a while and then sleep. But then, when their bedroom doors were shut, I would go to my bedroom, hop on my bed, and open the Word of God and try to read. Yes, try. It was difficult to read when your eyes are full of tears. I couldn't utter the prayer. I used to start with, *"Oh Lord, thank..."*, and choke up. I said my prayers in my heart and let the tears roll out. This went on for nearly four years. In the course of those four years, my husband and I stayed together and moved out, then circumstances bought us together, and then we moved out again.

Now through this entire journey, my husband was always with me, but it wasn't enough for me. He always said to me, *"I love you. Isn't that enough?"* and honestly it wasn't enough for me. I was brought up with the thought that, *"It's a woman's job to keep the family together"*. So, I felt responsible for breaking up the family. I blamed myself for separating my husband, the son, from his family.

One day, there was a huge fight, and the family decided that we both are not right and hence needed to be outcasted. It was at that time, my husband had a crazy travel schedule, and he had to be in the U.S., while I had to live all alone. I spent days crying and asking God, *"Why Me?"*

I was so angry, I fought with God all the time. I blamed Him for my existence itself. All I wished for was that the Earth just cracked open, I would fall into it, and it would close. I was embarrassed to meet friends as I was very proud of being in a joint family. I could not tell my family anything as I had done an inter-caste marriage. I could not tell them that the guy I chose was right but what came along didn't fit well, either that or I was just not a good daughter-in-law. That would imply their upbringing had failed.

I did not know what to do or whom to go to. I literally and truly felt alone. I felt unworthy and undeserving. I hated myself. I didn't look in the mirror for days, and when I did, I got so angry that I just started throwing and breaking things.

I broke out screaming and crying out loud. I felt so hurt that I was on knees all the time, looking up and asking God, *"Why? I would never hurt even an ant intentionally, so where did I go wrong? Is loving people wrong? Is sacrificing wrong?"*

I had changed myself so much to fit in that I didn't even remember who I was anymore. And if I did everything that was needed to make everyone happy, why is everyone still unhappy with me, and I am unhappy too? It was a vicious circle of life I was on. God being my witness, only I know how many times I considered suicide. That seemed like it would be easier than suffering this heartache.

And after months of misery, I gave up. My prayers moved from, just crying to surrendering. I said, *"God, I know You are there. You may be hiding now, but I know You will not forsake me because that's not Who You are. So, I surrender. Show me the way."*

This went on for months.

One day, I got up, and I had this amazing feeling inside of me. I felt something had shifted. I decided to make some nice masala chai for myself. While the chai was boiling, I had an epiphany.

"When you change the way you look at things, the things you look at change".
~ Wayne Dyer.

I asked myself, *"Am I looking at this all wrong?"* I was this fabulous, confident, and witty woman – before I got married. So, what changed? Did I let the thoughts and questions of others change my way of viewing the world?

Now I was curious. First, I was curious about where this quote popped up from. I think it was God's way of answering my question by giving me more questions.

I decided to try it out. I started it with stepping out. I began meeting friends again and got back to work.

I was now cleaning my glasses through which I saw the world. It wasn't easy, those glasses had become clouded and dirty. I needed the right cleansers to make it happen.

I decided to find the right ingredients. Now I was on a mission. A mission to understand how and why things happen the way they happen. I think when we are ready, the Universe/God, some Power greater than you, guides you and gives you exactly what you want.

A little fast-forward... Let me tell you what I learnt.

I discovered that it was my beliefs that worked against me:

- Elders are always right.

- A woman is responsible to keep the family together.
- A woman should follow the rules set by her in-laws to live her life.
- A woman should never raise her voice, no matter how incorrect/unjust things are around you.
- Once a woman is married, she has nothing to do with/for her family.

Now changing beliefs doesn't come that easy. However, when you see your beliefs for the false friends they are, they lose their power.

I started small. The first step I took was:

#SochBadalneSeHiHoga – Change Your Thoughts – Change Your World

But it wasn't easy. I was in danger of falling back quickly. So, I decided to do something that would remind me every day to keep at it. I got myself a tattoo – "Princess" – daughter of the Almighty King – God. It acted as a reminder for me every day.

Walking on the path of editing one thought at time and one belief on my time – I was able to now convert my belief to:

- Age doesn't define wisdom.
- I am responsible for only my happiness.
- A woman should live by her own rules.
- You have a voice. Use it for the betterment of self and the world.
- The beliefs that hold someone back are no truer than the beliefs that spur someone into positive action. So,

it makes sense to choose to focus on the beliefs that get you the great results you want.

- Freedom is not given to you. You have to claim it, own it, and not give it away.
- Thinking Positive always isn't naïve – it"s just better.

In the last three years, my relationship with myself and my family is better than ever. I am a much happier person. I am a changed person. I am no more working on others but working on myself. I wouldn't say I have got it all and I am always in a positive state. I think unless mentored by a Buddhist or Zen Master for years, I will have a lifelong journey with this one.

I am taking one day at a time, changing my thoughts to change my world. I am now responsible for just my happiness.

"When you get to a place where you understand that love and belonging, your worthiness, is a birthright and not something you have to earn, anything is possible."
~ Brene Brown

I have realized that the feeling of belonging is not something that you can find outside of yourself. If you love yourself and accept yourself just the way you are, you don't long to belong to a family, society, or external world. More than anything, you've got to belong to yourself. It is in a true sense, a change that you establish from the inside out. During my many years of experience, whether with myself or my clients, I have learned that any change that is inside out is a long-lasting change.

#SochBadalneSeHiHoga – Change Your Thoughts –
Change Your World.

I have to be honest. That's one of the things I always address with my clients whether coaching business or writing. Today, I am a successful business coach, a writer's coach, an author, and a publisher. Now you may be wondering, *"How does the sense of belonging impact work?"*

Trust me, it does. When you start your work/business/entrepreneurship – whatever you may call it or do, the fact remains that you want to feel accepted in your field whether you are in essential oils, jewelry design, health products, life coach or any business that you run. You are looking at being accepted by your audience, your clients, your competitors. You desire to be the best in the field by feeling a sense of belonging.

You may be surprised, but the truth is most of the entrepreneurs enter a new business without giving a thorough thought/study/research before they even jump in. For a few, it works just great, however for many, it doesn't. One of the many challenges that I see these new entrepreneurs or even coaches, for that matter, face is feeling overwhelmed with what they see their competitors do. Most of the times, it's about being successful as soon as possible. Social media also plays a role in it. Everything is online and immediate. I see many entrepreneurs feel intimidated with things like:

- How others are getting high paying clients where they are not moving forward at all;

- How others are getting more followers or likes than them;

- How to be a six- or seven-figure income person as soon as possible.

Now, while we talk about delayed gratification being less valued by the next generation, I feel it's true with new entrepreneurs too.

I see the desperation of getting returns on investment at the earliest and in the battles of feeling belonged, accepted, and successful all at once. The decisions are hasty, the moves are all over the place, the message isn't clear, and eventually, nothing seems to be working. And in this, I personally, as I expressed earlier, have experienced and seen clients fall back to the questioning and doubting self. This is where I follow what I learned.

Business or entrepreneurship definitions have changed over the years. Today, it's about being a brand. In my book *I Work for Me*, I talk in detail about how one can learn to be a brand.

Your business/work needs you 100%. By that, I don't mean 24/7, I mean even if you are working just two hours a day for your business, it needs your 100%. If you are broken, bitter, have huge baggage, your business will suffer. This is what I help my clients with. I help them find their belongingness by taking one step at a time. I have seen my clients not only change inside out but achieve some remarkable goals in their life and work. As this process is the core of my work, I like to call it the "HEART.

H – Heal Yourself

E – Engage

A – An Action Everyday

R – Regularity – Staying Consistent

T – Thoughts Create your World

It may sound cliché, but the ultimate truth is to belong. You need to be ready to let go.

If you have read anything on Law of Attraction or follow the science, you know that the more attached you are to the outcome the more you delay it.

While healing is always spoken only about past traumas and big disappointments in life, I believe that healing is an everyday process. We experience various emotions every single day, and they need to be processed, and what's not needed has got to go to help us move forward.

Now, it is definitely a process, and considering the space here that I have here to explain, I would want to leave you with just one thought if you are wondering, "Where do I begin?" I say:

#SochBadalneSeHiHoga – Change Your Thoughts – Change Your World

I believed that I can, and I did it. I continue to do it, and I will continue to accomplish my dreams.

Yes I can! …and you can too. I believe in you. Do you believe in yourself? I feel the sense of belonging to this world. Do you?

About the Author

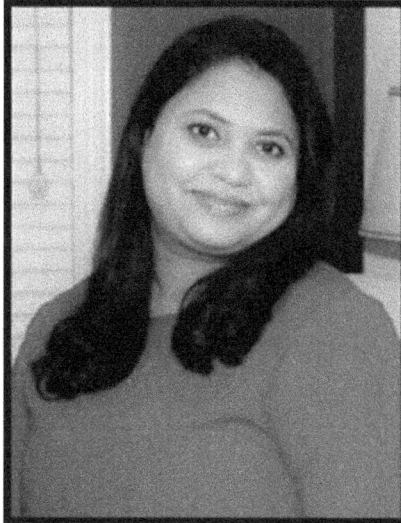

Snehal R. Singh wears multiple hats – author, publisher, coach, and speaker. She has mentored and coached more than 25 Certified Coaches establish their business of coaching and grow 5X through her program – Right to Abundance:

www.righttoabundance.com

She was also nominated as one of their Top 30 coaches in the U.S.A in 2019. Snehal has trained more than 1,000 coaches and helped them get certified as an ICF-approved Coach.

In 2019, Snehal completed her mission of helping 100 authors write, publish, and flourish. Her Signature Program, Be an Authorpreneur, is a complete guide to write your first book, publish it, and grow. She has helped more than 18 authors complete their first book in 2019. Her clients come from all parts of the world: U.S.A., U.K., Canada, India,

Australia, Cameroon, Nigeria, U.A.E., Malaysia, Thailand, Germany, France, and more.

Snehal's best-selling book, *I Work for Me,* is loved and appreciated by entrepreneurs and coaches. If you want a copy of her next book, *An Essence of Soul: The Art of Serving & Mindful Cooking,* absolutely free, email her the receipt of the purchase or transaction-ID of this book to:

info@snehalrsingh.com

If you are looking to expand your business and voice your message through a book or writing, connect with Snehal now. Book an Appointment at:

www.snehalrsingh.com

The Power of Shooting Your Shots

Tequila Cousar
Certified Life Coach, U.S.A.

"You are only one shot away from living a completely different life."

~ Tequila Cousar

The Unthinkable

If I told you that I quit my job as a dental hygienist to be a full-time mom to my newborn daughter with no financial backing, would you believe me?

When I was 19, I was told by my family physician that I had no chance of becoming pregnant. I was deemed infertile due to anovulation. This condition is when a female's body doesn't produce eggs. As a female, can you imagine getting the news that you cannot do one of the most important jobs that you were sent on Earth to do? This totally crushed my spirit. My mother was beside me the day I received this awful news. She refused to accept this outcome, and we scheduled an appointment with another doctor. Upon examining my situation, she stated that the outcome of me becoming pregnant was possible. All I needed to do was take a pill that will allow me to create a monthly menstrual cycle, but she admitted that my condition was abnormal.

Those pills sent me into all types of hormonal whirlwinds. Some days I was happy, sad, or even just mad for no reason. I hated the way they made me feel, but I wanted to be sure that I was doing everything right.

At the age of 21, while in dental hygiene school, I met my husband who is a dental assistant. He totally swept me off my feet with his charm and warm personality. We would talk about marriage, owning a business, and children. I told him that it was my dream to be a stay-at-home mom. We both wanted it so badly to come true.

Three years later in 2004, we got hitched! What a beautiful day! I graduated from dental hygiene school the year prior to our wedding and things were going as planned – well, at least that is what we thought.

We started trying to have children immediately because we had a plan, but after seven years of doing the baby dance, we were unsuccessful. We had spent thousands of dollars on infertility meds and 70+ pregnancy tests. I was exhausted, and I just wanted to die! I couldn't believe that it was happening, but then again, I could. You see, remember that I was told by my family physician that I couldn't have children? Well, it is said, "The first impression is a lasting impression." Although we had a second opinion, my first physician's words stuck with me. They were looming in my mind. This was when I noticed how depressed I had become. I was mentally abusing myself and emotionally eating. I weighed almost 230 pounds!

I was not happy. I had to do something different.

I started praying, meditating, and reading self-help

books. Little did I know this would change the course of my entire life, my self-talk, my diet, and my outlook on life.

After two years of consistency, I miraculously became pregnant! I took five pregnancy tests that day to confirm that this was really happening. Yep, I was going to be somebody's mama!

After embracing my pregnancy, which is one of the most amazing journeys that I could have gone through, I gave birth to my daughter in 2011. One look in her eyes, and I knew that I never wanted to miss any of her "firsts," so guess what? After 12 weeks of unpaid maternity leave, I returned back to my job and turned in my two-weeks' notice. Yep, this girl just quit! Honestly, I was overwhelmed and burned out mentally, physically, and emotionally with my job due to repetition, and I was hitting the glass ceiling.

I had no plan of how I was going to support my family financially, just an idea.

Eight years after the "Big Quit," I could not could have imagined that today I would be a Certified Life Coach, business consultant, author, master motivational speaker, and home-school educator. This could not have been possible if I did not tweak my mindset.

Becoming who I am today was half the battle. Read on because there is more to this story.

The Conflict

"How are you going to make money?"
"You are just going to waste all of those years of college."
"Being an entrepreneur isn't a real job."

Those were the words that came out of associates', friends', and my family's mouth when I told them that I had quit my job to pursue my dream of becoming a "mompreneur."

Those words almost made me think that I had done something wrong – as if I had made the wrong decision. Have you ever made a decision that was best for your family, but because of other people's opinions, you started to question it? Yep! We all do something that is against the grain, but in order to break the mold of our families' generational curses, we have to create generational blessings.

In college, I was exposed to my first real business. It was a work-at-home business, and I was selling legal insurance. I was pretty good at it. I used the money I earned to pay for books and food. I loved the fact that I could help other students who were strapped for cash. However, they were likely to become discouraged when they didn't make a sale. So, I would encourage them to keep going and to dig deep and know why they were doing it, and the money started flowing in.

Because of my success with this enterprise and years later, after quitting my job, I joined a home-business and within the first year, I became a Top Seller, ranked such four times, and earned lots of prizes and cash. But after doing this for five years, I was burned out, and it wasn't bringing me joy.

In 2016, I learned about personal branding and how to attract potential clients by focusing on educating and inspiring others based on what I knew. This is also the year that live streaming became a thing, and I started doing live videos about shifting the mindset.

And this is how I knew what I needed to do to marry my love for business and personal development.

The Breakthrough and Lessons Learned

Poor planning, mindset, and other people's opinions are the top three issues that affect want-to-be and emerging entrepreneurs today. I could have let my family and doctor's opinion rule my life, but I didn't. I had to see past their opinions and do what was best for my family and me, and that was to think and be different.

To create a positive mindset, it takes work! You have to be consistent in your vision and what you believe. Many people don't want to start a business or see what else is out there because they are too afraid to take any chances. I thought about the risk and failures that come along with becoming an entrepreneur, but the promise of the gain of freedom, learning lessons, and expanding my zone of genius helped me to become resilient.

So, If I told you that It is possible to quit your job or even go part-time to focus on your genius, would you try it? I know it sounds too good to be true but remember that any and everything you believe is possible. If you believe that bad will happen, it will. If you believe in the greater good of all things, then good will happen. You just have to pick sides and stick with it.

Despite my journey of misfires, there were a few factors that kept me pushing forward, which landed me in the position that I am in today. These are some of the biggest secrets that I have learned from my journey:

1. Ditch the limiting beliefs that have been implanted in you by those around you. Someone has told you a lie about who you are, and you believed it. They have never served you, and they will never serve you.
2. Believe that "I can, and I will!"
3. Surround yourself with people who can fuel your desires.
4. Let go of negative people in your life.
5. Create a plan! Start with a 30/60/90-day plan.
6. Know that you are bigger than your job. You have an innate gift that is waiting to be unleashed. You just have to get quiet and listen.

The Ordinary World

I grew up in the inner-city of Dayton, Ohio. My father worked as a building attendant for the Dayton International Airport, and my mother had two jobs as a waitress. I have three sisters, and we got along for the most part. Sometimes we would argue over the usual things such as wearing each other's clothes without asking or what to watch on T.V., but other than that, my parents wanted us to focus on being a unit. From what I could remember, we would spend most of our weekends at our grandmother's house with our cousins, aunties, and uncles. The house was pretty cramped, so we would sleep wherever we could.

The moment that changed things for me was, at the age of nine, my parents divorced, and my sisters and I were blindsided. We all were deeply hurt because they both hid their pain; we did not see this coming. My mom got full custody, and after the divorce, so we barely saw our father. My mom was left to raise us four girls. She did the best she could with what she had and what she knew, but there were strict rules.

The one thing that my mother instilled in us was that it is important that you make yourself a priority and teach others how to treat you. Although we were raised in an environment where kids are to be seen and not heard, loving who we were and putting ourselves first was important.

I was the underdog, and I felt like the "black sheep" of my family. I was the middle child that people knew but did not see. I do not want to say that I was invisible to my parents when I was younger, but what I can say is that I wasn't their favorite – but I knew my parents loved me.

I was bullied from elementary through high school. My escape from all of this was reading books that made me feel good. I can remember being a six-year older who loved staying in the library for hours since we lived right across the street from it. This had both a good and bad effect on me, I think.

Good, because I loved reading mystery books. I guess it was the sheer illusion of solving a complex problem. As a late teen and even now, I love self-help books. I mean, it is an addiction, and I love reading anything that will make me become a better person. Because of this, I have become such an empathetic, caring, kind person who always has the vision to evolve.

Bad, because books were an escape from reality. I had an issue about speaking up for myself. I am much better about today, and I am daily getting better. Being this person caused me to have some quiet powers.

Here is what I know for sure: I knew from a very young age that I would be good at inspiring people and running a business because of how it showed up in my playtime. I just had to figure out how to marry the two.

The Call to Action

In 2016, while vacationing with friends in Miami, I was sitting in my hotel waiting area alone. It allowed me to really think about how I wanted to make an impact in this world. This was when I decided to become a life coach. I always felt that this was my purpose and where I belonged.

I immediately signed up with an online program and became a Certified Life Coach!

As an introvert, I figured that I had some quiet strengths when it comes to people and business. I shine with people I connect with because I show up from a place of curiosity, gratitude, and authenticity. I am patient, kind, and a good listener! I help them see the big picture quickly. I can give them steps on how to break down complex things into small steps, and I feel like their "accountability buddy"! I love doing this, and it comes so naturally.

I joined a Mastermind Group Coaching program on marketing online. I wanted to stay in my lane of motivating and inspiring others, but I wanted my niche to focus on women professionals who were burned out and overwhelmed in their careers. So, I created my coaching program, helping women who are overwhelmed and burned out in their profession to stay motivated and inspired as they build their brand online and offline around what they love to do. You can find more information here :

www.tequilacousar.com

Believe me when I say in the beginning, not everyone is going to buy into what you believe. And that is okay! Not everyone is going to be your customer. There are people who are out here waiting on you to unleash your gifts. You just have to "shoot your shot."

Here is what I did to identify my purpose:

1. I knew that I had a gift that needed to be unpacked, so I hired a coach to help me unpack and package it. What skills and talents do you have buried that need to be uncovered?

2. Sometimes you have to just shut up! You can learn so much about yourself and others when you listen. I believe that meditation is a key ingredient to understanding your purpose.

3. I knew that I had a message that was bigger than me, and I needed to share it with others. Your story is the key to opening peoples' hearts – and wallets.

4. I focused on what I am naturally good at and monetized it. What comes naturally to you?

5. I invested in myself. Investing in yourself is one of the key components to leveling up as an entrepreneur. How will you invest in yourself this year?

The best part about focusing on what I love doing and helping others is my clients are getting outstanding results:

- Diona made an appearance on *The Doctors* TV show sharing her story.

- Pat started a business focused on marriage, and now she is traveling around the world empowering other women in their marriages.

- Yolanda was a burned-out professional who has now embraced her love as an occupational therapist and started her own senior-living facility that she runs from her own home.

- If you are feeling overwhelmed and burned out in your profession and ready for a shift, schedule a free 30-minute, one-on-one consultation with me at:

www.tequilacousar.com.

The Growth and Brightness of the Future

With over 400 million entrepreneurs worldwide and with the expectation of 27 million Americans who will leave their traditional workforce in favor of full-time entrepreneurship by 2020, there is no doubt that becoming an entrepreneur has been the goal of so many people around the world.

Yes, your life will be busy, but at least you will be busy doing the things you love. The confusion comes when you ask yourself, *"What should I be doing?"* Trust me, I know that feeling, but I know the steps that will get you into calling your shots so that you can work on your terms and live in a future that is created by you.

I packaged a portion of my coaching session into an e-book. This allows me to focus on being strategic with my time as well as my clients.

Here are some products/services, besides my one-on-one coaching sessions, that I created to help you have more success:

- **Shot Caller Business Plan Blueprint**, you can find it on my website:

  www.tequilacousar.com

  The steps in this ebook are often missed by most professionals starting their business online. It is not enough to have a pretty website and a logo; you need a plan.

- **"Pick My Brain" Session**. This is a 60-minute session where I use a unique hybrid of consulting and coaching to provide insight, strategy, and guidance. During these sessions, you can ask me any questions related to the specific situation. You can book here:

  https://tequilacousar.com/pick-my-brain/

The Reward

Since 2011, I have not had to be stuck in rush-hour traffic, my daughter doesn't have to stand in line for the school bus, and I don't have to go to a job that I hate. Creating this ideal life that I had wanted since I was a child allows me to be a home educator for my daughter.

After my daughter turned eight, I decided that I wanted to return to my career as a dental hygienist, but I wanted it on my terms. So, I applied for a contingent position at our local hospital and scored it! So, I work there when I want, and I still get to work my business from home.

I have the best of both worlds when it comes to home and my career.

I have been featured in multiple, digital publications such as *The Huffington Post*, *Nia Magazine*, and have spoken on many stages.

I wonder where my life would be now if I didn't believe in myself, God, and taking a risk – but I do!

The Wisdom

- You only live once, so try new things and create new experiences.
- Money doesn't always have to be the goal when leaving a legacy. Showing your children how to take a calculated risk can be a very valuable inheritance.
- Be clear on what you want, where you are going, and write it down.
- Don't get stuck in the "compare and despair" trap. Everyone's journey is different. Focus on finishing your own race.
- Make it until you make it. You don't have to fake a life you want until you have achieved it. Create the life you want, one step at a time, until you make it.

"You are not designed by a title but by purpose."
~ Tequila Cousar

Peace and blessings,

Tequila Cousar

Power Summary

Let's do a quick recap so that you can grasp the key concepts:

1. What are the three top issues that affect want-to-be entrepreneurs?
2. Identify your star power. What makes you shine?
3. What is the best investment you will ever make?

Success Actions

Here are three success actions that you can take right now to make things happen in your career:

1. If you are an overwhelmed professional, Identify what you would like to do next.
2. Identify what you need to remove from your life in order to start new things that are aligned with your purpose and bring fulfillment.
3. Write down your 30/60/90-day plan. If you need help, email me at:

<u>intoxicatingheartsllc@gmail.com</u>

About the Author

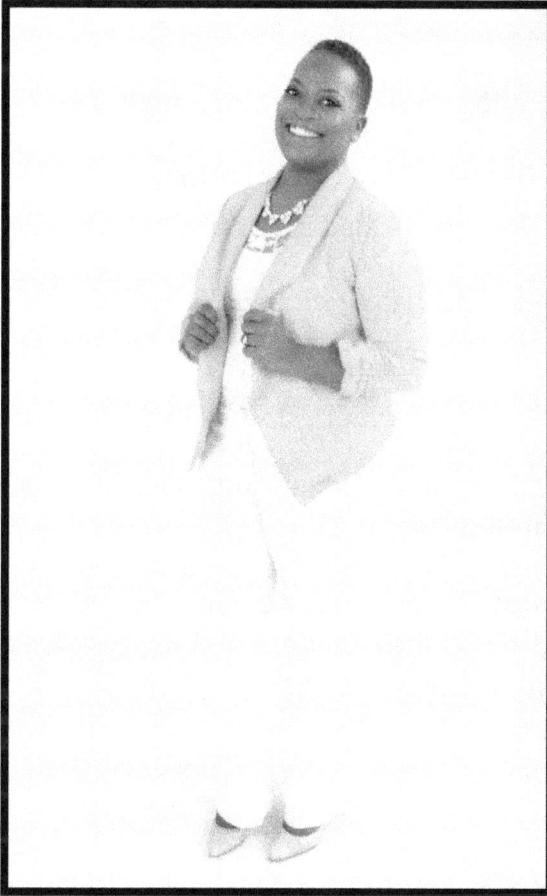

Tequila Cousar resides in Columbus, Ohio and is a proud wife and mother of two. She is the owner of Intoxicating Hearts, LLC. She is a Master Motivational Speaker, author, Workshop Facilitator, Certified Life Coach, and Registered Dental Hygienist who specializes in personal branding and business consulting. She is a graduate of The Ohio State University and Central Michigan University.

Business Name: Intoxicating Hearts, LLC

Website: www.tequilacousar.com

Email: intoxicatingheartsllc@gmail.com

Facebook: https://www.facebook.com/tcousar1

Facebook Group : Shot Caller Revolution
bit.ly/shotcallerrevolution

Instagram: https://instagram.com/tequila_cousar

Linkedin:
https://www.linkedin.com/in/tequila-cousar-377165a/

Services: Coaching, Consulting, Digital Products and Motivational Speaker

Ideal Clients: Professional women who are overwhelmed and burned out in their careers and ready to take the leap into entrepreneurship.

A Mother Who Trusts

Tracie Osborne
Certified Life Coach, U.S.A

Specializing in Mindful Parenting

"'Be here, not there."

~ Tracie Osborne

The Unthinkable

One day in the middle of my son's behavioral episode and my resulting outrage, I realized that the traditional parenting method does not work for this child. Whenever I yelled at him and gave him a command, it just made him more defiant. He would refuse to listen. He would refuse to move. He would shut down. I would lose control and yell and threaten him. I would then give him harsh or corporal punishment.

The first time I laid eyes on him in Jan 2011, I saw his head, and I got a feeling that something was not right. I brought it to his pediatrician's attention, and he told me, *"His head is growing faster than normal."* He referred him to a neurologist within the first weeks of his life.

The neurologist ran tests and scans, and everything came out negative. He said, *"Your child just has a big head."*

Apparently, it runs in the family because they wanted to run tests on my sister's head until they saw my mother's head.

His behavior progressively worsened. By the time he was three years old, I had exhausted all of my resources. I didn't know anyone who could relate to what I was going through, so I sought professional help. His evaluator stated that he has been doing this type of work for over 20 years and that he recognizes when kids need help. He said that my son needs to be in a special school that knows how to handle kids like this. Although I innately knew something was off from the very first time I saw him, it wasn't until this moment that the acceptance of this reality crashed on top of me like a ton of bricks.

Then, the weight of shame and guilt set in with a barrage of flashbacks of comments and conversations by teachers and behaviors that I myself witnessed; the things that have always stuck out, but I had always ignored. His preschool was right. A year prior, his preschool had recommended he get evaluated after my son bit a child on the face, threw furniture, and spit at the teacher. I denied the evaluation. I said that it was just "terrible twos." He had just had tubes placed in his ears to help the fluid drain from his ears. His doctor explained that his hearing had been muffled during the primary years of his speech development. This is the reason he has a speech delay, and that's the reason he is expressing himself physically.

But little did I know that a year later, an evaluator would tell me that indeed he needed help. The evaluator told me that my son needs to be in a classroom with no more than eight students and two teachers. Once he is enrolled in that school, he will have a special bus take him to and from school.

It was on a Wednesday afternoon with clear blue skies. I went to visit the school that the evaluator recommended. The school was based in a house that was converted into a school. I met with the administrator, and she gave me a tour. She first showed me the music room which was in a different house from where we met.

We walked to the house and climbed the steps, and I opened the front door. I suddenly felt pounding in my chest, and the room started to spin. I gripped the door handle, and my hand slipped off from the sweat that now covered my body. I took my fingers and rubbed my eyes and looked straight ahead only to realize that I was not dreaming. I inhaled and exhaled deeply and took a step into the music room.

There were eight students in the room with two teachers, including the music teacher. The children were in a semi-circle singing along with the music teacher. Most students were bound to wheelchairs with bibs draped over them, and others wore helmets. The music teacher was wearing a striped shirt with thick glasses, and she was playing the piano which was draped around her neck and was rocking from side to side, singing along with the kids.

I didn't have 20 years of experience, but I knew that the school was not a good fit for my child. I knew that at three years old, if my son was placed in this environment, he would mimic the other kids' behavior and get worse. I decided to let him remain in the preschool he was in and have the services that he needed to be provided at the school. But the services did not help when he was out of control at home. I didn't have a service that I could call when I couldn't handle him. I thought if I self-healed myself from suicidal thoughts and depression, I could figure out how to manage my son's behavior as well.

I saw a parent posting on social media that she had started her journey to 365 days of no yelling. She also had four boys like me. It sparked some interest in me. I joined her challenge because yelling was not working for my son. I tried for a while, but I failed miserably. I couldn't make it through a day without yelling at one of my four boys. I felt shame and guilt. I knew that yelling didn't make things better, that it scared my boys, that it shames my kids, and that it doesn't teach my sons how to do better. And even though I knew I wanted to change, I would resort back to yelling because that was what was normal.

On a school night in May of 2014, I was getting my four boys aged nine, six, and three-year-old twins ready for bed. All of them had taken their baths and were settling into bed, except for my youngest. He sat on my bedroom floor and refused to move. I tried everything to get him to listen from yelling to corporal punishment, but none of it worked. It became apparent to me that the traditional way of parenting just did not work for this child.

After about two years of discovery, I figured out how to control my son's challenging behavior without yelling and giving harsh punishment. In the interim, I taught him how to control his behavior as well. Then, I thought if I could remain calm when dealing with my most behaviourally challenged child with learning disabilities, I would be able to do the same for all four of my boys. I have not yelled or given harsh punishment to them ever since. If it wasn't for my son, I would still be parenting in the traditional way. At the time, I didn't realize it, but I became a "mindful parent."

Anything is possible as long as you believe.

If I told you that years later, embracing my son and his

challenges have helped me to create a successful business, would you believe me? If I had given up and placed my son in a special school, I wouldn't have been able to build a successful business, a "no-yelling" movement, and work with the most amazing parents around the world.

You don't always get your version of the perfect child. All you can do is love them and accept them for who they are.

The Conflict

I thought I mastered the inner voice or what I like to call "The Inner Bitch." I gave the inner voice a name over 15 years ago when I realized that it was the cause of my depression and suicidal thoughts. I couldn't give her a name like "Mary" or "Jane" because they did it no justice. I would lie in my bed in a dark room in a fetal position with no appetite, and all I would hear was

"I am ugly."
"I will never amount to anything."
"I am a failure because I don't know what I want to do for the rest of my life."
"I am skinny."
"I don't deserve to live."
"I have this college degree, and no one is hiring me."
"I have failed in life."
"I have failed my parents."
"I followed all the rules and still failed."

I listened to those thoughts for hours, days, months, and years until one day, I realized that no one was telling me these things. It was all coming from "The Inner Bitch."

I faced myself in the mirror, and I said, *"You will no*

longer hurt me! I will get to understand you and teach what I have learned to others." I became obsessed, so that's what I did.

Unbeknownst to me, that was the start of my conscious-living journey. But then, I was faced with challenges with my son, and my parenting skills were tested, and it started again.

"I am a bad parent because I can't control my son."

"I did something wrong to cause his challenging behavior."

"I don't deserve to be a parent."

"I have to give harsh consequences, or he will get worse."

"I am the reason he acts like this."

"I didn't sign up for this."

"I am all alone."

After some time, I realized that I was hearing the exact same voice that caused me so much misery and pain. The only difference is that it is making me feel like a bad parent.

When I became aware that the same thing was happening. I looked at my reflection and said, *"You had me fooled, but not anymore!"* And that was the start of my "mindful parenting" journey, and the experience and lessons I learned along the way are all a part of my online success. I love teaching mindful parenting to parents. You can visit my website at:

www.tracieosborne.com

If you only had an idea of how many mental roadblocks I faced while getting my business going, you would be pleasantly surprised. I want to share with you the wisdom and lessons I've learned from those years of struggle so that you can use adversity as a powerful tool for the greatest achievements in your life. So, when you think that I could never be successful, you will rephrase that and say, *"Yes, I can do anything I put my mind to."*

In order for change to happen, you have to believe in yourself before you have physical proof. Are you ready? I feel that you are. I believe in you, and now it's time for you to believe in yourself and your capabilities. Repeat after me:

"Yes I Can."

The Breakthrough and Lessons Learned

What made dealing with my son difficult was the parenting beliefs that I had. Whenever my son would become defiant, I would think,

"I am the parent."
"He is supposed to listen."
"He is testing me."
"He knows how to push my buttons."
"He knows what he is doing."
"He is doing this to get his way."
"It is my way or the highway."
"A child needs to stay in a child's place."

It was all the beliefs from culture and society that were bestowed upon me. Those beliefs caused me the most misery and suffering because I believed that was the only way to parent.

It was becoming aware of these thoughts that had the greatest impact on my reactions towards my sons. I realized I had the power to choose what thoughts I was going to listen to. I no longer reacted; I responded to my sons in a positive way.

I learned that thoughts are just suggestions and that I didn't have to believe every thought that comes into my mind, and that most of my thoughts came from beliefs that came from an outside source. Those beliefs no longer aligned with the kind of parent I was striving to be. I changed my parenting mindset to fit the parent I was becoming.

The other big factor was that I had four boys that were looking up to me. They were learning how to deal with their emotions based on my reaction to them. Whenever I would feel the need to have an outburst, I would remember that I have an audience that is watching and learning from my actions. It was my duty to be an example for them.

On my 10+ years business journey, I had tremendous support from family, friends, accountability partners, coaches, and consultants. Yes, I learned a lot of hard and expensive lessons and invested in a lot of business ventures , but it shaped me into the person I am today and the success that I have in my business. Having the tools and accountability from those who have been in your shoes helps tremendously on your path to success.

Here are the key factors that I used on my business journey:

1. Know your "why." Why do you want to help others? It has to be something beyond material gain. It has to include things that are priceless. On your journey to success, it will get hard, and you are going to want to quit. If you have a strong "why," it will help you through those hard times.
2. Get rid of the beliefs that don't align with your vision.
3. Stay focused on your target.
4. Have a "support and accountability team." Be certain to choose people that are like-minded.

5. There will be times when your support system is unavailable. It is important to be able to self-motivate.

6. Always be kind to yourself when you make a mistake. Forgive yourself easily.

7. Be self-aware of thoughts and emotions. Most of how you operate is done on autopilot. You are making decisions based on the way you were raised or by the beliefs of others. In order to make a change, you have to make a conscious effort.

8. Once you are aware, you will be able to observe the impact that your thoughts and emotions can have on your success.

9. Self-analyze when something doesn't work out the way you planned and write/record it in a journal.

10. Embrace failure. You learn your biggest lessons from it. You learn how to do better by doing it the wrong way. In order for you to learn the best way that works for you, you have to experience what doesn't work for you.

The Ordinary World

I was born and raised in America, a fast-paced country full of culture, ethnicity, and social norms. My father is from Trinidad and Tobago. My mother is from the U.S.A. I am the eldest of three sisters.

My parents used the traditional way of parenting to raise us. It was the social norm. They were parented in this way themselves, as well as their parents.

I was taught to be respectful, follow the rules, and get good grades. If I failed to follow the rules, I got a negative consequence.

I never had a need or a worry growing up. We went on a lot of family trips. I have the best parents a girl could ever wish for, and I wouldn't change it for the world.

The Drama

In 2015, I had a near-death experience, and in the midst of it, I had an awakening. It was through that experience I became aware of something so much greater than me. I was grateful that I got a second chance at life because I am able to fulfill my purpose of awakening human consciousness. I was not quite clear on how I was going to do it at first because I had self-healed and was self-taught, and I was unsure of how to label what I did.

What was always clear, though, was that I had a purpose to fulfill.

I spent five days in the hospital recovering from bilateral pneumonia. I got home, and I was overtaken by emotions. It was the first time my boys saw me since I was admitted to the hospital. The way they embraced me and cried on my shoulder was like they knew they almost lost me.

I remember sitting in the living room on my couch and watching them play without a care in the world. I was mesmerized by their ability to live in the moment. I learned a lot from them that day that life is simple and that I need to stop making everything a big deal and to live mindfully and enjoy life.

The Call to Action

I realized that part of my mission was to teach others what I learned on my journey. By the end of 2015, I gained two Life Coaching certifications. I created a beta program and took the data that I received and created my online course. I realized I needed help with an online business system.

I invested in a business program that gave me an online business system. I spent about six months learning the system. My biggest struggle was not the system; it was me. I was in my own way. I second-guessed myself all of the time. I cared about what people thought of me.

Once I got out of my own way and I believed in myself and my capabilities, I was able to see clearly and figure out the problems, pain points, and challenges that people faced.

I combined the knowledge I gained in my 10-year entrepreneurial journey and started my online business.

I use social platforms to guide parents on yelling less and being more present so they establish a greater connection with their children. I knew some of the biggest problems parents faced with was being overwhelmed, fatigue, and frustration. They have other areas of their life figured out, but when it comes to parenting, it is a challenge. They never dreamed they would be a yelling mom. They never intended on parenting the way their parents parented them.

Most parenting is done unconsciously based on your own childhood experiences, culture, and society. I created the "5T Mindful Parenting Method" to teach parents how to parent in a mindful (in the moment) way. It is not just a program that packs you with a lot of info; it is a lifestyle change.

You can find more information about this at:

www.tracieosborne.com

Do parents say that it is in their nature to yell? Yes. Do I take it personally? No. I understand that there are two types of people – or in the words of Confucius,

"Those that think they can and those that

think they can't are both usually correct."
I only work with those that think they can change.

Here is what I reflect on when they say they can't:

1. I don't take what they say personally. It has nothing to do with me. It's when you take things personally that makes it harder to move on.

2. I am an example of what I teach. I show it on social media. A person has to see you seven times before they even consider buying from you. So, it's important to show up every day and be an example of what you teach. A seed will be planted, and they will come when they are ready.

3. I keep in mind that some people are not ready for what I have to offer.

4. I know my worth and the value I am able to share.

The best part of my work is being a part of my clients' parenting transformation.

Semoy lives a mindful lifestyle.
Kathy is yelling less.
Sara has a better relationship with her children.
Kelly self-healed from her childhood trauma.
Morgan has less stress with her kids in the mornings.
Val is aware of her triggers.
Jane is parenting the way she always imagined.

If you are seeking to become a 5T Mindful Parent, schedule a free 20-minute strategy call at:

www.tracieosborne.com

From my experience, I have started a no-yelling campaign to bring awareness to the negative effect that yelling and harsh punishment has on children, and the effect it has on them when they become an adult.

It is time to break the cycle of yelling out of frustration, and time to use a more mindful approach of teaching kids how to deal with their negative emotions.

The Growth and Brightness of the Future

It was a beautiful Saturday afternoon when I was meditating, and about halfway through my one-hour sit, I heard my son storm into my bedroom. He saw me sitting on my bed, meditating. My boys do not disturb me when I am meditating. He started breathing hard as he paced back and forth. I wondered what happened to him. I was prepared to break my meditation to assist him. Then I remembered that I had promised him a bag of his favorite chips (Takis). I forgot to go to the store and get them.

When he gets frustrated, he usually throws anything in sight and will take his frustration out on his brothers. I was prepared to break my meditation to control him if he escalated. He left my bedroom leaving everything in place.

He walked by his brothers and went downstairs. After a few minutes, the air filled with a burning smell. I started to think about what he could possibly be doing. As I was about to go and see what he was doing, I heard my older son ask him what he was burning. He came upstairs and the smell got stronger. His older brother asked him, *"Why are you eating burned popcorn?"*

After my meditation was complete, I called my son into my room. I stooped down to his level and told him that I was proud of the way he handled his frustration. He did an excellent job. I told him, *"I noticed that you were filled with a lot of negative emotions, and you didn't react to them. I know you wanted your chips, but you saw that I was meditating you chose not to disturb me – and you got a snack and patiently waited for me to finish."*

We held each other tight as tears filled my eyes and streamed down my cheeks. After a couple of minutes, he ran towards his brothers full of excitement and blurted out, *"Mommy said that I did good and that she is proud of me!"*

Seeing how excited he was warmed my heart with so much delight. I got myself together and got his chips from the store.

He was a little over seven years old. I knew that everything I fought for was worth it, and my decision not to put him in a special school, have him labeled, and put on medication was all worth the triumphs. I am not against any of those services. You must know your child and know what's best for them. In my child's case, these were not necessary.

I have since created many programs for parents to help them yell less and be more present. I get overjoyed when I see my clients' transformations as they become the best parents they can be. Here are a few of my programs that have helped many parents across the globe:

- **5T Mindful Parenting Method** – Skills and tools needed to become a mindful parent.
- **5T Conscious Living System** – Tools to help people along their conscious - lifestyle journey.
- **5T Mindful Mama Tribe** – A group filled with like-minded mamas.
- **Meditation Made Easy** – Gives the tools needed to work through the beginning stressors of meditation and provides insight on how to meditate for more than 15 minutes.

- **No-Yelling Movement** – A campaign that brings awareness to the negative effects of yelling and harsh discipline.
- **1-on-1 Coaching** – Helping parents directly with their specific parenting needs. It's like having my Mindful - Brain on call.

If you want to know more about my work, you can email me at:

guidance@tracieosborne.com

...and we will talk, or you can follow me on *Instagram* or *Facebook* @tracieosbornespeaks.

I am excited to be working on my mission of the No-Yelling movement. I am looking forward to more interviews, campaigns, and whatever else is destined for me.

I'm looking forward to collaborating with other like-minded entrepreneurs and to be a part of the 5T Mindful Parenting journey of so many parents.

The Reward

Every day, I pinch myself to make sure that I am not dreaming. I am so humbled that I am able to live the life that I always envisioned. I have freedom of time. I am able to pick and choose my schedule. I no longer need permission to go on vacation. My business is online which means all I need is a laptop, cellphone, and Wi-Fi to do business. I am the PTSO (Parents Teacher Student Organization) Co-President at my middle schooler's school. I have the time to be involved in all four of my sons' three schools. I am able to take a 10-day meditation course yearly where there is no talking, no cellphones, and no communication with the outside world. I am a mental health advocate. I love helping others and giving back to my community.

Dark times are inevitable. It is the lessons learned in those times that will give you your greatest achievement. We live in a world of duality. There are going to be good times and bad times. It is the way you perceive those bad times that gives you your experience.

Embrace what is, because nothing lasts forever.

The Wisdom

I have gained a lot on my journey to success:

1. Darkness is there to help you get stronger.
2. You have the choice to turn "The Inner Bitch" into "The Inner Supporter."
3. Thoughts are just suggestions. You don't have to listen to every thought that comes into your mind.
4. Give your thoughts an identity so that you are no longer dictated by them.
5. Be mindful of your thoughts and emotions.
6. Believe in yourself and stop worrying about what others think and are doing.
7. Get out of your own way. The only thing that is stopping you from success is you.
8. Stay in your lane and show up as the best version of yourself. There is no competition. There is no other person that thinks and perceives the way you do.
9. Have lots of patience.
10. Believe in yourself, claim it, and take aligned action.

"The mind is your most powerful tool.
Master it and the world will become your

oasis."
~ Tracie Osborne

All the best to you on your journey,

Tracie Osborne

Tracie Osborne

Certified Life Coach Specializing in Mindful Parenting

Power Summary

Let's do a quick review:

- Be aware of your thoughts and emotions;
- Learn from your failures;
- Have patience;
- Believe in yourself;
- Journal;
- Meditate.

Success Actions

Here are nine steps that you can take today to be successful in your business:

1. Be conscious of your thoughts and emotions. You can contact me at:

   guidance@tracieosborne.com

   ...if you need help.
2. Focus on one task at a time.
3. Believe in yourself.
4. Stop comparing yourself to others.
5. Stop worrying about what others think.
6. Stop second-guessing yourself;
7. Be consistent;
8. Be your number-one fan;
9. Journal.

About the Author

Tracie Osborne has a revolutionary approach to mindful parenting and conscious living. She provides online programs, coaching, workshops, retreats, and online communities. Her personal experience and education in Mindfulness have given her a broad base on how to solve an array of problems. She especially likes working with mothers for whom the traditional way of parenting is not working for their child. You may learn more about her services at:

www.tracieosborne.com

Business Name: Tracie Osborne

Website: www.tracieosborne.com

Email: guidance@tracieosborne.com

Facebook: www.facebook.com/tracieosbornespeaks

Facebook Group:
www.facebook.com/groups/318467758778891

Instagram: www.instagram.com/tracieosbornespeaks

Services:
- 5T Mindful Parenting Method
- 5T Conscious Living System
- Meditation Made Easy
- 5T Mindful Mama Tribe
- 1-on-1 Coaching
- No-Yelling Movement
- The Beginners Guide to Meditation

Ideal Clients: Parents who want to yell less, be more present, so they establish a greater connection with their children.

This is dedicated to my mom and to all the parents who can relate to my story.

Sustainable Strategies

Dr. Wahidah Hashim
International Researcher, Malaysia

"There is no beauty in writing a research grant proposal without really understanding the main issues to solve."

~ Dr. Wahidah Hashim

The Struggle

When I first joined the university, I had been working in an industry. I left the industry to pursue my career in academia, more or less, because of the thought that I can "roadmap" my own work to what I wanted to do. But joining university was totally a challenge. The multi-tasking jobs demanded of you are tremendous. There are times you have to prepare the lecture notes, teach new subjects, mark the answer sheets, and on top of that, you need to bring money back to the organization by securing research via grant proposals.

Sometimes you also need to secure consultancy projects as another way of generating income. Among the hardest tasks for me, and I believe to everyone else as well, is securing money for the university. You need to know what it is worth so that people will be willing to invest their money for you to do something for them. This is similar to research grants. You need to be able to craft a good proposal in order to convince the funder that it is worth funding for the project, and at the same time, you must do research that is useful and meaningful to others. Another challenge is when you have secured a research grant, you need to be able to run and manage the project with limited resources since it is most likely a task-specific kind of work. This is even more challenging when the support system in the university is very limited.

The Challenges

Writing a proposal is not an easy task. Strangely, despite the workshop and the training they provide you to prepare for the proposal, you still do not really understand how to find a problem. When you know what the problem is, then you must convert the problem into a project that is worth funding, prepare a reasonable budget, plan on how to run the project with limited resources, produce outcome that meets your clients' expectations, and then strategize the entire project so it is sustainable for the funder as well as satisfactory to the proposer.

When I first started writing a proposal, I started with just a small, internal, university funding grant. The proposal was prepared with only a literature review done over the Internet and other resources from books. I never interviewed those who were actually involved in the areas that project that I proposed.

Maybe at that time, I just did this for the sake of my annual job performance rather than not having any achievements in this area. My proposal was accepted, but running the grant turned into a failure. I only managed to utilize 10% of the amount that the university. It was my fault that I did not spend enough time on thoroughly going through the ideas and prepare reasonable deliverables. I also did not read the guidelines, so did not understand the meaning of each of the many, many clauses. Because of this, I felt a bit deflated, and just had no motivation to apply to new any proposals at that time.

Real Experience

My first four years at the university, I was struggling to write a proposal. The research grant activity was just something that is strange to me if the theme of the proposed project was familiar to me. I also did not know what to propose and how to deliver a good project for them. I can just say that I was lacking in inspiration, so I just wrote for the sake of submitting a proposal.

It turned out that I was not the only one struggling. Few other colleagues, even they have been many years in the university, experienced the same difficulties. During my fifth year at the university, I started to learn the techniques of writing a proposal. The techniques, when tried, happen to work, and I managed to write 10 proposals within a year and secured all of them.

Obviously, all this was also dependent upon the research grants, there were some easy ones and there were some difficult ones. Despite being easy or difficult, we need to write a very good proposal that is worthy of funding, even it is just US$1,000. After all, although securing a large dollar amount for a research grant is important, what is more important to me is to propose something that has an impact and value to the funder, society, organization, and myself.

While securing the grants, I found that a lot of time as a project leader was spent in managing the grant instead of doing the real research that you are passionate about. As a researcher, you need to be good at the subject under research. You cannot be bogged down with administrative tasks. Oh, how I wish everything could be managed via some artificial intelligent, clerical robot so that I could concentrate most of my time in the real research.

As a project leader, you need to be able to manage your project resources such as research assistants (RA). Recruiting an RA is really a risk. You can only rely on their resume, recommendation, and your own instinct. Those RA who have a passion for doing research may be less challenging compared to those without.

I had an experience with an RA whereby they just quit without telling us that they quit and did not want to pursue their Master's or Ph.Ds. The regulation is a bit loose so that you cannot sue them for all the money and salary that they have been paid. The contract does not at all specify what would happen if some of the staff quit, or at least the contract should require them to pay back the money they were given. This is a risk and improvement that the university should make.

Crafting a Research Problem Statement

A friend of mine used to say, in research, knowing the problem is good. All I can say is a problem is worth its value. When we read and research what problem to solve in the research proposal, we need to be able to understand it. Okay, fine – we can just *Google* it over the Internet and compile and assume the same problem in our local situation. This is not easy work since you need to read a lot and make sure the problem fits with your local situation. A problem can be more interesting if you make a visit to a situation by asking people and having informal discussions with people in order to understand it more. Through this indirect survey, you will understand the problem better and be able to tailor it to your own unique situation. "Unique" means the problem could be the same throughout the world, but it is slightly different in certain places that make it unique to propose a solution.

Believe me, it is this uniqueness that you will define your draft that presents the problem better in your proposal.

Converting Problem into Something that Is Worth Funding

How can you make it important and worthy of funding? First of all, you need to know if this one of the pain points of the funder. Depending on the funder's purpose of advertising the research grants, I can basically identify three types of funders:

1. A funder that just needs to spend the money for the sake of spending, like an endowment fund, and you can do any topics that try to solve some problems.
2. A funder that wants you to solve a problem that they are facing, so they know what the problem is, and they just need help to solve it.
3. A funder that invests some money for future expectations and wants to be at the very front of something.

We need to be able to identify who the funder is, and what type of research project that they are looking for. Sometimes you have very good research findings, but they just not interested in listening to them if they do not understand and appreciate what you are doing unless it really applied and related to the project they are looking for. Sometimes they do not know how your piece of work is connected to their problem, but if you see any value, you should be able to extract their issues and then explain how your research work can solve their problem.

Do Simple Budgeting

If you are new at research, I always encourage you to start small so that you have gathered experience in a small scale version. Try to ask for funding within small capacity, lead the project, and manage the research project well. It is also easy to do budgeting and costing and try to deliver in a timely fashion. Then, try to make it impactful, even it is just a small thing to do. Maximize the budget into something that you can develop a service out of that later on when it is not in use after the project has finished.

When I do budgeting, it depends on what is allowed and not allowed from the funder of the research grant. So, do read the research grant guidelines. In normal practice, it should start with resource salary, research materials, any travelling costs, consultations, exhibitions, patents, etc.

How can you prepare the budget if you are on a small-sized research grant? The answer is prioritizing things that are most important for you to deliver your own project and try to budget for a shorter project period that is within a three to six months period. When you are done with the project, try to apply for a higher funding, and by now, you already have an experience of how you can best plan for your budget.

Maybe for the research materials, you can ask around for quotations and make contacts with various vendors that can supply your research materials. As I wrote earlier, I will try to construct a budget that is not only useful to the project, but also something that can be used later as a service, or something that you can train others to increase their competency.

How to Run the Project with Limited Resources

When your resource is limited, to deliver the project outcomes, break your project into small tasks. Maybe, in the beginning, your project plan is not as efficient due to a lack of experience. But that is okay; do not be too hard on yourself. Break the big tasks into smaller tasks, target something small, and plan for something that can be accomplished within your limited budget and time. In my experience, managing small deliverables can help us deliver something doable and less stressful. But you have problems managing small projects, you will forever be unprepared for big ones.

How to Produce Outcomes that Meet your Clients' Expectations

In meeting the clients' research project expectations, we need to ensure that we understand what clients want and that that is clearly stated in the project deliverables. Again, break the project up into small sections so you are clear on things that you need to deliver. Plan something that is doable, and if it is not something that you have the skill to do and if it is important to achieve a research project outcome, try to outsource it or make it as a consultation.

There are some busy clients who have no time to read your thick project report. They just need you to present. During the presentation, try to prepare a visual or graphical representation. It is helpful for them to absorb the findings in a short period of time. If they require detailed information, they may refer to your report. I found many times that my clients are very busy, and they only want to hear what they want to hear. But sometimes I do put relevant, extra information in for me to highlight findings from the work they have sponsored or funded. My clients are happy with such extra reporting, and they will tell you new ideas. This is considered premium information for you to write another proposal.

How to Strategize the Whole Thing to Make it Sustainable

Plan to buy something that is useful after the project is finished. When you get your problem statement, try to break it into many categories. When you have contacts with the subject under study, try to keep in touch for other times. The opportunities for doing impactful research are not easy to get. You need to evaluate how your research findings are of value to people, so you need to be in contact with the people and see in what way your findings can be useful to society.

Another method to keep it sustainable is to ensure that you can divert your new skills into new ways that can help generate new research proposals or eventually skill that people will pay for as a service. Just develop your skills, although people pay you cheaply in the beginning. You need to make your resume and track record, as well as your skillset, full of competency that can be used in another project.

Another activity is writing a book. Out of your work, with your clients' permission, you could write a book and honor them as one of the authors or contributors. You will be surprised to see that, most of the time, you can get good projects because of trust and long-term relationships with clients and good job performance.

When you do research, you involve people. You need to be able to communicate and keep in touch just to take care of the relationship and make the project more efficient

On my last note, securing and managing a research project is challenging, but I strongly believe if you break it into small tasks and gain experience gradually, you will be able to carry out the work effectively.

Good luck with your projects!

Dr. Wahidah Hashim

"Study, plan, execute, and do your best; whatever it is, you have learnt something!"

~ Dr. Wahidah Hashim

Dr. Wahidah Hashim

Power Summary

- What should you do when you start to write a grant proposal?
- How can you plan for a sustainable research grant project?
- What did I do to structurally prepare a grant proposal?
- What should you aim for to ensure your research project is suitable?

Success Actions

- Look around and find any problem that can be an idea for your grant proposal. Write it down.
- Keep things simple, doable, focused, and impactful.
- Benefit from discussions and talks to gain premier information.
- Contact me at:

  wahidah.hashim@gmail.com

About the Author

Dr. Wahidah Hashim received her Bachelor's degree in Information Technology, Business Management and Language from the University of York, U.K. She received her M.Sc. degree in Multimedia Technology from the University of Bath, U.K., and her Ph.D. in Telecommunication Engineering from King's College London, U.K. She has been with the Institute of Informatics and Computing in Energy (IICE), Universiti Tenaga Nasional in Malaysia as an Associate Professor since 2016. Wahidah is a trainer at the International Malaysia Training Centre and a volunteer at Malaysian Technical Standard Forum in drafting technical codes for the telecommunication industry.

She has been actively involved in wireless communication research with nearly 100 publications and filed several patents on her research findings. Wahidah has secured several government grants as well as industrial grants. She has been on one of the evaluation panels for research grants since 2017. Wahidah trains engineers in network radio planning for cellular networks as well as unlicensed spectrum bands. Recently, she was invited to an international conference as a professional facilitator for young researchers in helping to strategize their research. Wahidah is very keen to help other researchers who are still new in their job, and she can be contacted at:

wahidah.hashim@gmail.com

Business Name: WH Creations

Website: http://iice.uniten.edu.my/people.html

Email: wahidah.hashim@gmail.com

LinkedIn:
https://www.linkedin.com/in/wahidah-hashim-265147141

Services:

- SILARA for signal assessment device.
- Consultation on preparing an accepted research proposal.
- Training course for Unmanned Aerial System Safety Management.

www.ingramcontent.com/pod-product-compliance
Lightning Source LLC
Chambersburg PA
CBHW022051210326
41519CB00054B/309